J2EE Simplified

J2EE Simplified

A Practical Guide to J2EE Project Technologies for Project Managers and Other Non-Developer Team Members

Gregory John Powell
and
Jennifer Wewers

iUniverse, Inc.
New York Lincoln Shanghai

J2EE Simplified
A Practical Guide to J2EE Project Technologies for Project Managers and
Other Non-Developer Team Members

iUniverse books may be ordered through booksellers or by contacting:

iUniverse
2021 Pine Lake Road, Suite 100
Lincoln, NE 68512
www.iuniverse.com
1-800-Authors (1-800-288-4677)

ISBN-13: 978-0-595-36979-9 (pbk)
ISBN-13: 978-0-595-81386-5 (ebk)
ISBN-10: 0-595-36979-0 (pbk)
ISBN-10: 0-595-81386-0 (ebk)

Printed in the United States of America

CONTENTS

CHAPTER 1

Introduction

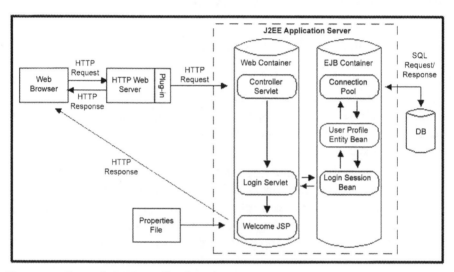

Figure 1-1: Example J2EE Application Flow

This book is for project managers responsible for the development of Java 2 Platform, Enterprise Edition® (J2EE) Web applications.

There are many challenges to successfully completing an application development project. A project can fail when team members do not reach a common understanding of business requirements or when the effort needed to complete the plan is underestimated. Issues can also arise with the statement of work, scope creep, change management, staffing, and a multitude of other things including the technology used on the projects themselves.

To help avoid these issues, strong project management and good communication among all team members is essential. It is possible to avoid many of the misunderstandings that can arise between team members by simply ensuring that all team members have a basic understanding of the technical aspects and terminology of the J2EE project.

Based on the illustration in Figure 1-1, *J2EE Simplified* will help you better understand the technology and terminology involved in J2EE applications, and avoid some of the miscommunication that can result in troubled projects.

By the end of this book, you will have a better understanding of the technology involved in building J2EE projects. With this knowledge, you will be able to minimize the risk of troubled projects by helping to ensure that all team members, not just the technical members, understand the technology used in a J2EE application.

Understanding J2EE Project Technology

When non-technical members of a project team do not have a basic level of understanding about how a J2EE application works, it can be difficult to set and manage expectations regarding the technology and to ensure its correct and effective application.

An example of this is the use of existing J2EE assets to create an application. Using existing assets help developers avoid writing much of the application code from scratch. Development teams can leverage two types of existing J2EE assets on projects:

- o **Company Intellectual Capital Assets:** In any company there is likely an inventory of propriety intellectual capital assets developed on previous projects. If a company has existing J2EE applications running in production, there are likely J2EE assets (pre-written and tested code) that your development team can leverage when creating J2EE applications.
- o **Open Source J2EE Assets:** Many of the technologies used on J2EE projects are available as no-cost, standardized open source intellectual capital available for download from the Internet.

Reusing J2EE assets leverages previous development investments, reducing project time and cost by eliminating the need to write and test this already proven code. Project managers who understand this aspect of J2EE can plan for the leveraging of existing assets in their project plans and application development.

Summary of Chapters

The chapters in this book present a top-level view of the technologies involved in developing J2EE-based applications.

o Chapter 2 provides a simple explanation of the flow of a Web page across the Internet.

o Chapters 3 and 4 illustrate how J2EE developers use Unified Modeling Language (UML) diagrams as the basis for creating their Java programs. If the Requirements and Design efforts do not create UML diagrams, your developers will have to perform Object-Oriented Analysis and Design while they are also trying to code the application.

o Chapters 5 through 13 explain the Internet flow when a J2EE application server is involved. These chapters discuss technologies including open standards, open source code, Java, HTML, XHTML, XML, Java Servlets, Enterprise JavaBeans, and JavaServer Pages.

o Chapter 14 explains deploying your code onto a J2EE application server using an EAR file.

o Chapter 15 concludes with final comments about information covered in the book and a comprehensive list of technologies used when developing J2EE applications.

We hope that the information contained in these pages will provide a common understanding for managers to use when planning, developing, and implementing J2EE applications.[*] Project managers armed with this basic knowledge will be able to minimize many of the communication gaps that are often the cause of troubled and failed projects.

---

[*] We have endeavored to keep this book brief so that busy project managers and other non-technical members charged with building J2EE applications will be able to read it quickly. This self-imposed constraint prevented us from providing in-depth explanations of the Java programming language and the technologies involved in building J2EE applications. Fortunately, a detailed explanation of these technologies is not necessary for project managers who will not be doing the actual development on a project.

CHAPTER 2

The Internet

Key to any discussion of object-oriented and J2EE technologies is a simple understanding how the Internet works. This chapter explains the Internet by following the basic flow of a Web page request from a Web browser to the Web server, where the Web page is located, and then how the Web page sent back as a response to the Web browser.

Web Servers and Browsers

What is a Web server?

A server is a computer that provides services to other computers, hence the name 'server'. You are likely using different types of servers whenever you work in a business office.

Instead of having your computer use its own dedicated printer and hard-drive storage, the Print server and File servers illustrated in Figure 2-1 can provide these services. For example, when you send something to be printed by a shared printer in your office, a Print server manages (or services) the printing of your print request along with all the print requests your co-workers send to it. If you store a document in a place other than your own computer's hard drive, a File server provides this storage (or service) area. In these scenarios, your computer is the client to the services provided by these servers.

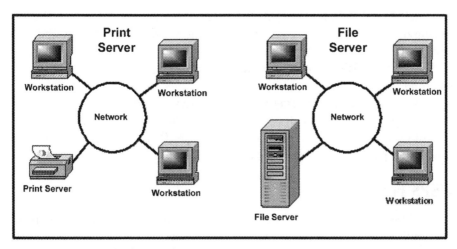

Figure 2-1: Print and File Servers

On the Internet, a Web server stores Web pages. As illustrated in Figure 2-2, when the Web server receives a request for a Web page, it services the request by sending the Web page back as a response to the Web browser. In this scenario, the Web browser is a client of the Web server.

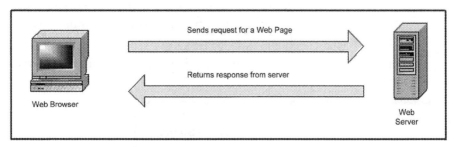

Figure 2-2: Web browser and Web server

What are Web browsers?

Web browsers are the graphical user interfaces (GUIs) that allow you to browse the Internet for Web pages. You could think of Web browsers as Web page requestors because their function is to request Web pages. When a Web browser receives a Web page, it receives it in the form of a Hypertext Markup Language (HTML) document. The Web browser uses this HTML to render, or display, the Web page.

There are many different Web browsers available on the market. The more popular ones include Microsoft Internet Explorer® (IE), Mozilla®, Netscape® and Opera®. While other devices besides Web browsers, like cell phones and

Personal Digital Assistants (PDA), also request and display Web pages, the following discussion uses the Web browser as the source of Web server requests and the destination of Web server responses.

How does the Web page request travel from a Web browser to the correct Web server on the Internet?

Explaining how the Internet and its underlying technologies work can be very complex. To simplify the concept, the following examples compare the system used by the United States Postal Service® (USPS) to deliver a letter to how a Web page request flows across the Internet.

USPS Flow

The USPS is an integrated system of mailing addresses, local post offices, main distribution centers, different transportation modes, and has rules that regulate how to send mail from one mailing address to another. For example, to send a letter, you enclose the letter within an envelope that meets the requirements of the USPS. As shown in Figure 2-3, mailing a letter requires the envelope to:

o Contain a destination address that specifies the delivery address of the letter.

o Include a return address that indicates where the letter is being sent from (not an actual requirement but if your mail cannot be delivered, the letter could never be returned to you).

o Have a postage stamp with the proper amount to pay for the delivery service.

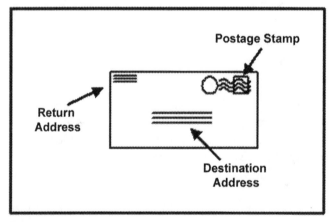

Figure 2-3: USPS Envelope Requirements

After enclosing the letter in the properly addressed and stamped envelope, the next step is to mail the letter. The upper section of Figure 2-4 illustrates the flow of a letter sent from San Diego to Atlanta.

o   The USPS letter carrier picks up the letter from your house and takes it to the local post office that services your postal address.

o   At the local post office, based upon your letter's destination address, your letter is forward to the main San Diego distribution center.

o   From there, using trucks as the transportation vehicles, the letter is routed to the main Atlanta distribution center, which forwards the letter to the local post office that services the destination address.

o   The letter carrier delivers the letter to the Atlanta address.

Internet Flow

The flow across the Internet is very similar to this USPS flow. The Internet is an integrated system of locations and transportation modes used to send and receive Web pages. Instead of using locations like postal mailing addresses, local post offices and distribution centers, the Internet uses locations with names like Internet addresses and routers. Instead of using vehicles for the transportation mode, a system of interconnected computer networks is used. Think of networks as the communications road that Web page requests and responses travel, similar to the streets and highways that the USPS trucks use to carry mail. Figure 2-4 contains a simple comparison of the USPS and Internet flows.

o   A Web browser (i.e., San Diego) sends the Web page request (i.e., your letter).

o   The request travels as a packet on the Internet.

o   The Web page request goes through a series of routers (i.e., local post offices and distribution centers) until it reaches its destination Web server (i.e., Atlanta).

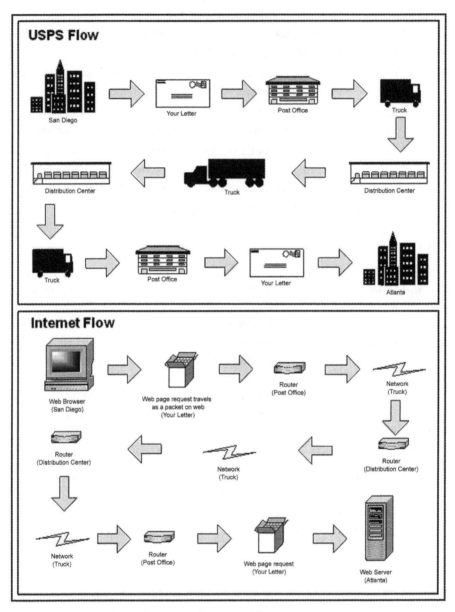

Figure 2-4: Comparison of USPS and Internet Flows

Addresses on the Internet

When a Web browser requests a Web page, it needs to find the address of the Web server on the Internet and then the location of the Web page on that server. In place of destination mailing addresses used by the Postal Service, the Internet uses the Uniform Resource Locator (URL) for its addresses.

Each Web page has a unique URL that the Internet uses to locate the page. Figure 2-5 shows the structure of a URL and how the URL finds a Web page. The syntax of a URL is actually very simple and consists of three basic components:

- o Server host name is the address of the Web server on the Internet.

- o Directory path is the location of the Web page on the Web server.

- o File name is the name of Web page as it is stored on the Web server.

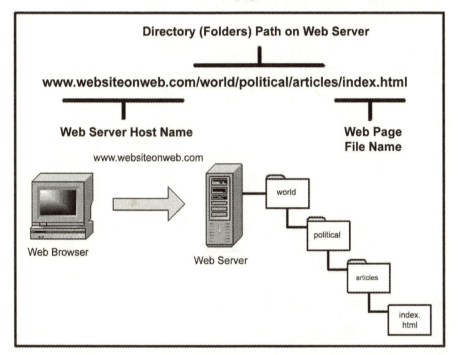

Figure 2-5: Uniform Resource Locator (URL)

In the example, the host name www.websiteonweb.com is the Internet address of the Web server. When the HTTP request finds the Web server, the server uses the directory path in the URL (world/political/articles/) to find the location of the file name index.html containing the Web page. The directory path included in the URL is the hierarchical directory path located on the server where the requested Web page is stored. When the Web server finds the Web page, the server sends the page back as a response to the Web browser. If the user only enters the host name, i.e., www.websiteonweb.com, a default Web page, generally the Web site's home page, will display. The URL's server host name can exist in one of two forms: Internet Protocol (IP) address and Domain Name System (DNS) name.

An IP address consists of four groups of numbers separated by periods, i.e., 255.255.255.255. These numbers make up the actual addresses of computers and many home Web pages for sites on the Internet.

For example, Google® is a very popular site on the Internet. If you were to enter the URL www.google.com in your Web browser, the home page of the Google site would display in your browser. You could also get the Google home page to display in your Web browser by entering its actual IP address of 64.233.161.104.

IP addresses can be difficult to remember. To make using the URL easier, the Internet allows you to enter a textual equivalent to the IP address, known as the DNS name. Entering the DNS name (www.google.com) is the same as entering the IP address (64.233.161.104).

Using our example URL, Figure 2-6 illustrates the difference between an IP address and a DNS Host Name.

IP Address Host Name:
255.255.255.255/world/political/articles/index.html

DNS Host Name:
www.websiteonweb.com/world/political/articles/index.html

Figure 2-6: IP Address vs. DNS Host Name

Domain Name System Servers

DNS-based URLs are great for people, but computers on the Internet require the numeric IP addresses. To resolve this issue, when a user enters a DNS-based URL, the Web browser first sends a request to a DNS server. The DNS server's function is convert the textual DNS host name in the URL to a numeric IP address. After making this conversion, the DNS server sends the IP address back to the Web browser as shown in Figure 2-7. The Web browser inserts the IP address as part of the Web page request. Now the request contains the actual IP address of the Web server where the Web page is stored.

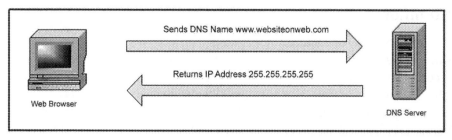

Figure 2-7: DNS Server

Routers

Once the Web browser receives the converted IP address from the DNS server, it forwards the Web page request to the Internet. The Internet uses a system of computer networks to pass or route the Web page request to the destination Web server.

To connect these computer networks together, the Internet utilizes specialized computers called routers. Routers connect two or more networks together and, similar to the distribution centers and local post offices used by the Postal Service, use the IP address to determine where a request should go next in its journey to find a specific Web page. Web page requests can pass through many routers along the way to the destination Web server. Figure 2-8 illustrates how routers connect networks together.

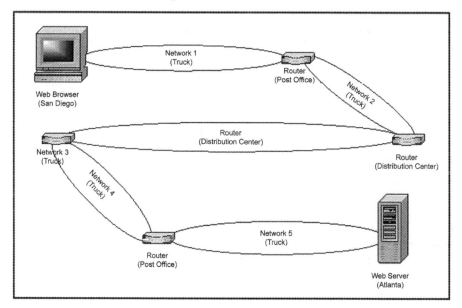

Figure 2-8: Routers Connect Networks Creating the Internet

Communication Protocols

For Web page requests and responses to move across the Internet, a set of rules is needed to allow computers on the Internet to communicate. This is accomplished by using communication protocols, which are a set of agreed to rules for how communication between different parties should work.

The Hypertext Transfer Protocol (HTTP) is the protocol used for Web page requests and responses. Because of their use of the HTTP communications protocol, Web page requests and responses are also known as HTTP requests and responses. The difference between HTTP requests and HTTP responses is that HTTP requests contain the URL for a requested Web page and HTTP responses contain the HTML used to create the Web page in the Web browser. For the remainder of this book, we will use the terms HTTP requests and HTTP responses in place of Web page requests and responses since these terms better define architecturally how the Internet works.

The HTTP communications protocol specifies certain rules for HTTP requests and HTTP responses. For example, one of the HTTP rules requires that destination and return IP addresses be included in every Web page request. Using these two addresses, the HTTP request can find its way to the destination Web server and the HTTP response can find its way back to the requesting Web browser. Another HTTP rule supports the Web page request to include the user's preferred language for displaying the returned page. Figure 2-9 shows how these HTTP rules resemble an envelope used to send a letter with the USPS.

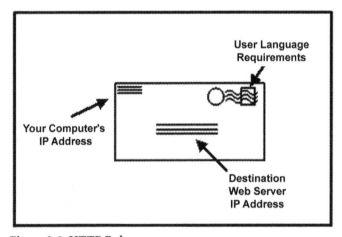

Figure 2-9: HTTP Rules

Any computer can communicate on the Internet as long as it uses a communications protocol supported by the Internet. The different communications protocols used on the Internet are included as part of the URL request allowing the Web server to identify the type of request. Since HTTP requests use HTTP communications protocol, an "http" is included as part of the URL to designate that these are HTTP requests. If you were to use the File Transfer Protocol, which is typically used to upload and download large files on the Internet, "ftp" would be included as part of the URL.

For HTTP requests and responses, even if the "http" is not included as part of the URL typed into the Web browser, the browser will add it to the URL before submitting it onto the Internet. Figure 2-10 illustrates the use of the HTTP protocol.

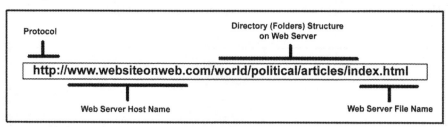

Figure 2-10: HTTP Communications Protocol Added to URL

Communication Packets

The HTTP communications protocol is used to identity the type of request, but HTTP depends on another protocol, Transmission Control Protocol/Internet Protocol (TCP/IP), to move the actual request across the Internet.

As we previously stated, when you mail a letter, the USPS requires you to place a stamp on the envelope to pay for the delivery service. If a standard weight letter requires you to use a 37-cent stamp, what happens if a letter weighs more than the maximum allowable weight limit? The Postal Service requires you add additional postage to the letter, for example, the postage could be 93-cents to mail the letter.

The Internet also needs to handle the issue of varying sized HTTP requests and HTTP responses. If lengthy HTTP requests or HTTP responses are sent that exceed the maximum length, for example, 1500 characters, there is no equivalent way to add postage on the Internet as the Postal Service requires for overweight letters. To address this issue, HTTP requests and HTTP responses are sent as fixed sized communications packets over the Internet.

If a lengthy HTTP request or HTTP response is sent, it is divided into a group of communications packets. Besides the usual information contained in HTTP requests and HTTP responses, each of the packets in the group is given a sequence number. For example, if a HTTP response was divided into three individual communications packets; packet 1 would be numbered 1 of 3, packet 2 would be numbered 2 of 3, and packet 3 would be numbered 3 of 3. See Figure 2-11.

When the three packets are sent on the Internet, they travel individually, even going through different network paths and routers before arriving at the destination address, i.e., the Web browser or Web server. Once the communications packets arrive, the packets' sequence numbers are used to reassemble them back into their original HTTP request and HTTP response formats. TCP/IP moves these packets across the Internet and assembles them at their destination.

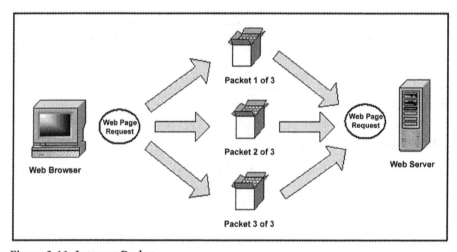

Figure 2-11: Internet Packets

Summary

The previous pages explain how a Web page request is sent across the Internet, finds the specific page, and returns to page as a response to the Web browser:

- o The user enters a URL in the Web browser to request a Web page.
- o If the user enters a textual DNS name as part of the URL, the Web browser sends the URL to a DNS server for conversion into a numeric IP address.

o   The Web browser submits a HTTP request for a Web page.

o   The HTTP request makes it way across the Internet through a series of routers as one or more communications packets until it finds the Web server containing the requested Web page.

o   The URL in the HTTP request is mapped to the directory structure of where the Web page is stored on the Web server.

o   Once the Web page is located, the Web server uses the return IP address included in the HTTP request to send the requested Web page back to the Web browser as a HTTP response.

o   The Web browser displays the Web page.

This simple flow is the backbone of all Internet-based applications. These may include corporate Web sites, Intranets, or any number of the Java applications used to conduct transactions and other business on the Internet or local Intranets. It is the basis for explaining how J2EE applications are developed.

CHAPTER 3

Object-Oriented Analysis and Design

There are numerous books written that explain Object-Oriented Analysis and Design (OOA/D) in immense detail. That is not the purpose of the next two chapters. Instead, the intent is to demonstrate how J2EE developers use the diagrams produced during OOA/D to create their Java code. These two chapters begin with a brief explanation of both the Java programming language and the Unified Modeling Language (UML), followed by explanations of UML Class Diagrams and the resulting Java code examples.

The examples illustrate how developers use UML Class Diagrams as the basis for creating their Java programs. Modeling your application in UML allows you to analyze and design your application before coding begins. In addition, the models guide your developers as well as your project plan by detailing:

- o The Java classes to be developed
- o The methods and variables to be included within each Java class
- o The Java class hierarchies structure
- o The Java variables and methods to be inherited from other Java classes when developing a Java class

Developers use the UML diagrams produced in the Requirements and Design phases to create Java programs. If the Requirements and Design phases do not produce UML diagrams, especially Class Diagrams, developers have no basis for creating the programs. As such, a J2EE project plan must support using OOA/D techniques.

In the object-oriented world, the tight coupling between OOA/D and OOP can significantly reduce the amount of code needed to write and maintain. The process of creating, analyzing and refining UML diagrams provide thoroughly analyzed and validated documentation required by developers to create a J2EE application that meets requirements, developed on time and on budget. Lack of validated OOA/D diagrams is one of the major reasons that too much code is written and re-written on J2EE projects.

Defining, refining, and validating the elements in the UML diagrams during Requirements and Design is important to the success of any project. Otherwise, the developers must create each class element during development—negatively affecting the project and causing budget overruns, missed deadlines, and cut application functionality to get the project back on schedule.[*]

OOA/D to UML to OOP

The primary programming language used to build J2EE applications is Java, which is an Object-Oriented Programming (OOP) language. Any OOP language implies that there are OOA/D techniques available to use during the Requirements and Design phases of a project that will set the stage for fast, efficient development of application code. One of these techniques is the Unified Modeling Language (UML). The UML diagrams drive a project's application development since your J2EE developers will use these diagrams to create their Java code as illustrated in Figure 3-1.

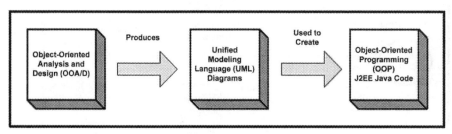

Figure 3-1: OOA/D to UML to OOP

Java Programming Language

Java is the core development language for creating J2EE Web applications. As a project manager, you do not need to know how to write a Java program. Nevertheless, there are elements within Java you should understand as part of managing a J2EE project.

---

[*] If you are interested in finding out more about UML, we recommend visiting http://www.omg.org/uml/

Java Virtual Machine (JVM)

Before Java, programming languages compiled their source code into a format understood by a particular operating system like Microsoft Windows or Unix. However, this meant the compiled code could only run on that specific operating system. Unlike other programming languages, Java developers can write a Java program once and then run this same code, without modification, on a multitude of different computer operating systems. (Figure 3-2)

For example, developers can develop and test their Java code using Microsoft Windows® and then deploy this same tested code on a Unix® server without any changes being made to the Java code to get it run on Unix.

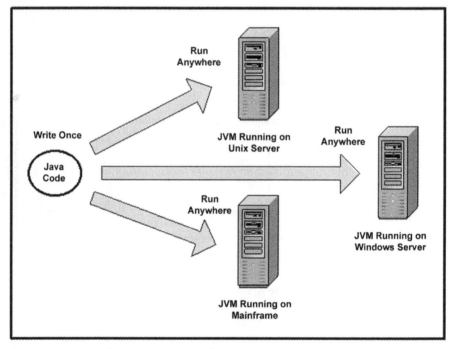

Figure 3-2: Java Write Once, Run Anywhere

As with all programming languages, developers write Java programs in a text-based format that they can read and understand. This is true of any programming language. The developers save their Java language programs in text-based files called Java source files. All Java source files end with a file type of ".java", for example, Order.java.

To execute Java source files, they must first be translated or compiled from the text-based format that the developers can understand into format that can be understood and executed by a computer operating system like Microsoft Windows or Unix.

Compiling Java source code creates compiled files called Java class files. All Java class files end with a file type of ".class", for example, Order.class. The Java class files contain compiled code called Java bytecode. Java class files do not run on a particular operating system. Instead, Java class files run on an imaginary computer, the Java Virtual Machine (JVM). The JVM executes the Java class bytecode and translates the bytecode into a format that a particular operating system understands. Any computer, no matter the operating system, that has a JVM install on it can run these same Java class files. The JVM gives Java programs their operating system independence. (Figure 3-3)

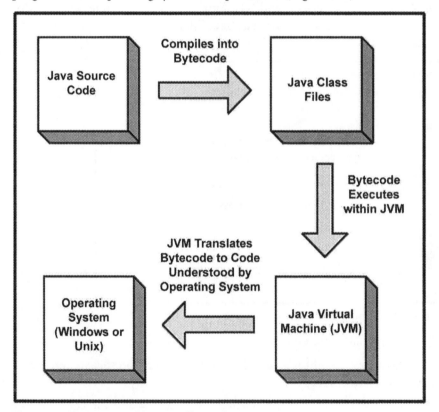

Figure 3-3: How Java Code Compiles and Runs

Java versus HTML

Java is a very powerful programming language and is the primary language used in developing a J2EE application. Like any programming language, Java allows developers to decide when and under what circumstances each line of Java code should execute and how often each line should execute. Java uses conditional statements to determine which lines of Java code should execute. A conditional statement evaluates to either true or false and thus, depending on how the statement is coded, will determine whether to execute certain lines of Java code or not.

For example, in the Java code snippet shown in Figure 3-4, the Java conditional statements "if," "elseif," and "else" are used to determine whether the driver of a car should drive through a street intersection based upon the color of a traffic signal.[*]

```
if (light == "green") {
        gas_petal = "foot on"; brake_petal = "foot off";
}
elseif (light == "yellow") {
        if (car_in_intersection == "true") {
                gas_petal = "foot on"; brake_petal = "foot off";
        }
        else {
                gas_petal = "foot off"; brake_petal = "foot on";
        }
}
else {
        gas_petal = "foot off"; brake_petal = "foot on";
}
```

Figure 3-4: Java Conditional Statements

The code in Figure 3-4 says:

o If the traffic light is green, then your foot stays on the gas and is not put on the brake.

o However (**ElseIf**), if the traffic light is yellow and the car is in the intersection, then your foot stays on the gas and not on the brake.

---

[*] (Note: The Java code examples in these two chapters contain only the snippets or fragments of code needed to demonstrate the example, not the complete code needed with a Java file to run the code.)

o But (**ElseIf**), if the car is not in the intersection yet, then take your foot off of the gas and put it on the brake.

o Otherwise (**Else**), the traffic light must be red, so take your foot off the gas and put it on the brake.

It is important to remember that Java is a programming language, while some of the other Web development languages discussed in this book are not programming languages. These languages, like HTML and XML, do not have the ability to control if and when specific lines of code execute. Unlike Java, there are no conditional statements like "if," "elseif," and "else" in HTML or XML. Therefore, every time their files execute, each line of HTML or XML code executes.

Java Classes

As mentioned earlier, Java source code compile into Java class files. A typical J2EE application can contain thousands of Java classes. Understanding classes can be a bit confusing. The reason for this is that the term "class" in OOA/D has a different meaning than it does in the Java programming. In OOA/D, classes correspond to real-world things or objects like Orders, Invoices, and Customers. A class in Java is an application program.

Developers use OOA/D classes defined during Requirements and Design to create a corresponding Java class during Development. This is the primary reason that Java developers require OOA/D be done before they create the application code. Otherwise, your developers will need to define these OOA/D classes while they are also trying to code them as Java classes. If the latter happens, your project is likely in trouble.

Unified Modeling Language

The Unified Modeling Language (UML) is the industry accepted standard technique for graphically modeling an object-oriented application. Being industry accepted enables object-oriented developers located throughout the world to understand the Requirements and Design of an object-oriented application modeled using UML. The terminology used for OOA/D and UML is technology independent, and as such, different Object-Oriented Programming languages can use OOA/D and UML diagrams to develop applications. Since the goal of this chapter is not to teach OOA/D or UML, we will discuss these topics in the context of Java development.

Java projects use UML to model applications through a series of diagrams with names like Class Diagrams, Sequence Diagrams, and Use Cases. Each diagram has a specific purpose and conveys different information about the application. For example, UML Class Diagrams provide a visual representation of the OOA/D classes defined during Requirements and Design.

UML Class Diagrams

In Object-Oriented Analysis and Design, everything revolves around the UML Class Diagrams. UML diagrams show both the OOA/D classes and how the classes relate with each other. Class Diagrams allow developers to see the scope of the programming needed to implement their Java classes. Developers use Class Diagrams to define and write Java application code.

An OOA/D class consists of two components: attributes and behaviors. Attributes represent data that can be stored about the class. Behaviors represent operations the class can perform. Behaviors access the attributes to perform their operations. For example, an Order has attributes like an Order Number or Type of Order, and behaviors like Display Order, which uses the attributes to display the Order.

An Order, therefore, is a class. All the Orders created by users of the application would be members of the Order class, since these Orders would have the same or common attributes and behaviors.

Figure 3-5 shows an example of one class shown on a UML Class Diagrams, though many classes can appear on a Class Diagram. A rectangular box divided into three areas represents a class on a Class Diagram:

o   Class name: the name of the class (e.g., Order)

o   Class attribute: the data that can be stored about the class (e.g., Order Number and Order Type)

o   Class behavior: the operations that can be performed against the data in the class (e.g., Display Order)

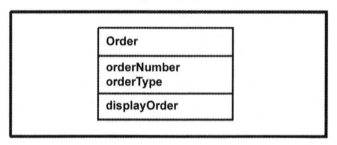

Figure 3-5: Class Diagram Rectangular Box

As we previously stated, developers write their Java class code using Class Diagrams. Figure 3-6 contains a snippet of Java code developed from the Class Diagram example shown in Figure 3-5.

```
public class Order {
        private String orderNumber ;
        private String orderType ;

        public void displayOrder ( ) {
                System.out.println("Order number: " + orderNumber) ;
                System.out.println("Order type: " + orderType) ;
        }
}
```

Figure 3-6: Java Code Developed from Class Diagram

Creating a Java Class

One of the first steps when creating an OOA/D class is to give it a name. The upper area of the Class Diagram rectangular box contains the name for the class. Figure 3-7 shows the first area of a UML Class Diagram rectangular box contains the name Order. We will call this the Order class.

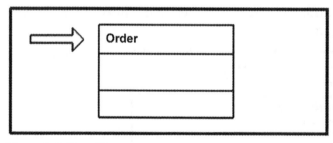

Figure 3-7: Class Name

A developer would use the OOA/D class name in the Class Diagram to write the Java class code as shown in Figure 3-8.

- o The code "**public class Order {**" signifies where the Order class code begins.

- o The closing "}" indicates the end of the code for the Order class.

- o The code belonging to the Order class would fall between the associated class braces. The code between/* and */are descriptive comments included by the developer to document the program and are not included when the Java compiler compiles the source file.

```
public class Order {
        /* Java code for Order class falls between the class braces */
}
```

Figure 3-8: Code to Create a Java Class

OOA/D Attributes become Java Variables

Attributes define the properties, or data values that can be stored about an OOA/D class. Another way of saying this is that attributes define the types of data values that can be stored about a class. For example, the Order class has attributes that distinguishes each specific occurrence, or instance, of the class from another. That is, each Order has a unique set of data values like Order Number and Order Type contained in its attributes that distinguish it from other Orders.

The second area of the Class Diagram defines the class attributes. In Figure 3-9, we have defined two attributes for the Order class. The attributes are Order Number and Order Type. Per naming conventions, the first letter in an attribute is lowercase with the first letter in every remaining word capitalized. For example, the attributes Order Number and Order Type become orderNumber and orderType.

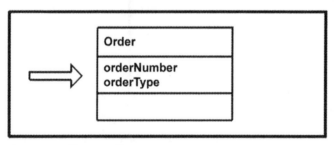

Figure 3-9: Class Attributes

When developers create the Java class code, they write the code for the attributes defined in the Class Diagrams. Java developers use the attributes captured on the Class Diagrams to create the Java variables in their programs. Figure 3-10 shows an example of the code that defines the variables in the Order class program. The code creates two text or String variables called "orderNumber" and "orderType."

```
public class Order {
        private String orderNumber ;
        private String orderType ;
}
```

Figure 3-10: Adding Java Variables to Order Class

The new code in Figure 3-10 creates two Java String variables named "orderNumber" and "orderType." String variables store alphanumeric text values. The data that is stored in these Java variables is what distinguishes one occurrence or instance of a class from other instances of the same class. In other words, the data stored about an Order instance differentiates one Order from any other Orders created using the Order class. For example, our example program will store six character values like "P00001," "W00002," and "P00004" in the Order Number variable. Each of our Orders can only exist as one of two Order Types, either a "Purchase Order" or a "Work Order." See Figure 3-11.

Name	**Value**
orderNumber	P00001
	W00002
	P00004
orderType	Purchase Order
	Work Order

Figure 3-11: Variable Names and Values

OOA/D Behaviors become Java Methods

The third area of the Class Diagram defines the class behaviors. Behaviors are the operations that OOA/D classes can perform. The naming conventions for behaviors are similar to attributes. The first letter in a behavior is lowercase with the first letter in every remaining word capitalized. Therefore, Display Order becomes displayOrder.

In Figure 3-12, we have defined a behavior named Display Order for the Order class. Display Order displays the data values in the Java variables. In a real application, an Order class would most likely have many more attributes and behaviors. For instance, an Order would likely need attributes like Shipping Address and behaviors like Create Order, Update Order, and Cancel Order.

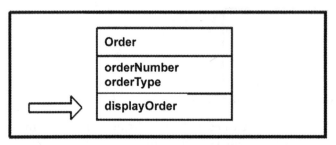

Figure 3-12: Class Behaviors

When Java developers create their programs, they need to define code for the behaviors in the Class Diagrams. Behaviors become methods in Java classes. Methods are the code that performs the operations using the Java class variables. Methods create, read, update, or delete data within these variables. Java developers use the behaviors captured on the Class Diagrams to define the needed methods for the Java classes. Figure 3-13 shows an example of the code that the developers could use to define the methods in the Order class program.

- o The line "**public void displayOrder()**" defines a Java method for Display Order. If any arguments or data is needed to be passed to the method, these arguments would be listed between the parentheses.
- o A method's code is contained between the method's beginning "{" and closing "}" braces. In this example, the method contains two lines of code that display the Order Number and Order Type.

```
public class Order {
        private String orderNumber ;
        private String orderType ;

        public void displayOrder ( ) {
                System.out.println("Order number: " + orderNumber) ;
        System.out.println("Order type: " + orderType) ;
        }
}
```

Figure 3-13: Code to Add Methods to Java Class

Encapsulation

In Figures 3-10 and 3-13, the words "private" and "public" are used in the front of the code that are used to define the Java variables and methods. Words like public and private are called access modifiers since they allow or restrict access to a variable or method. For example, public methods allow code from other Java classes to execute the methods while private methods hide the methods from access by other classes.

The words private and public are important to Java because they specify if other Java classes can directly access a class's variables and methods.

In the object-oriented world, using a private access modifier allows for a concept called encapsulation. Generally, encapsulation prevents one class from accessing methods and variables in another class. For example, encapsulation would prevent any method in the Invoice class from directly changing the value in Order Type from "Work Order" to "Purchase Order." Public methods within the Order class can only make these changes.

If the variables in Figure 3-10 had used the public access modifier instead of the private modifier, any method within any other Java class would have access to those variables.

For example, the Invoice class would be able to have direct access to the Order class's variables and could add, change, or delete the data in those variables. Of course, this would cause application development and maintenance chaos because you would not know how many Java classes in your application could change the value in a particular variable.

Therefore, class variables should be private. To allow a class (e.g., Invoice) access to another class's (e.g., Order) private variables, the methods contained within the class (e.g., Order) need to be defined with the public access modifier.

Figure 3-14 shows that public and private classes are indicated on Class Diagrams using plus (+) and minus (-) signs. The plus sign (+) marks the attributes and behaviors that can be accessed by other classes and the minus sign (-) marks the attributes and operations that cannot be accessed by other classes.

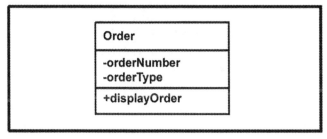

Figure 3-14: Indicating Public and Private Access Modifiers

Encapsulation, or "data hiding," hides private variables data behind the class's public methods. Figure 3-15 illustrates the concept.

The private variables orderNumber and orderType are located in the inner circle. You cannot access variables in the inner circle without first going through the methods in the outer circle. The outer circle contains the public methods, for example, displayOrder, that another class needs to use to access the inner variables.

In summary, defining a variable private restricts access to that variable to the code defined for that class. Defining a variable public opens access to that variable any other class.

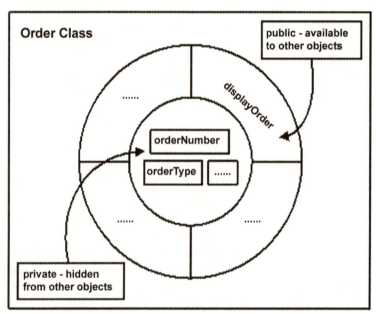

Figure 3-15: Public vs. Private Access Modifiers

Understanding encapsulation and access modifiers are important in the object-oriented world. A key component of your Requirements and Design efforts is determining how to access the methods and variables of each class.

CHAPTER 4

More OOA/D

The purpose of this chapter is to continue the demonstration of how the output generated from OOA/D drives a project's Java development.

In Chapter 3, we created an OOA/D and Java class. In this chapter, we demonstrate how to create instances, also known as objects, from a class and discuss class hierarchies and their use to facilitate code reuse.

Creating an Object from a Class

For code within a Java class to execute, you must first create an object or instance of the class. Creating an object is called "instantiating" a class.

A Java class is a template or blueprint for creating the objects or instances of the class. The Java class determines everything that an object does through its methods and stores through its variables. Once you create an object, you can access its methods and variables. Each class can create an unlimited number of objects.

Another way of thinking of a class and its objects is to think of them as a cookie cutter and the cookies created using the cookie cutter. The Java "class" cookie cutter can created many Java "object" cookies.

In Figure 4-1, the code in the Order class "cookie cutter" creates three Order instances "cookies". Once an Order object is instantiated, the data for that Order can be stored in a database.

- o Order instance 1 is used to buy Pens and has an Order Number of P00001.

- o Order instance 2 is used to buy Paper and has an Order Number of P00002.

- o Order instance 3 is used to buy Tape and has an Order Number of P00003.

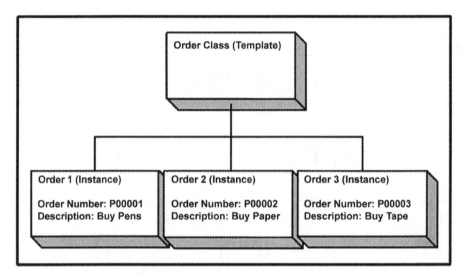

Figure 4-1: Creating Instances from Class

Figure 4-2 contains an example of how a developer could code the creation of an instance from the Order class. In the example, creating an instance of the Order class results in an object named newOrder.

o   The line "**Order newOrder = new Order()**" creates a new Order instance or object named newOrder from the class Order.

```
...
    Order newOrder = new Order( );
    ...
```

Figure 4-2: Creating an Instance from a Class

Executing an Object's Method

Once the developer writes the code to instantiate the newOrder object from the Order class, code can be written that executes any of newOrder's public methods. For example, to execute an object's method, the code must specify the name of the object and the method to execute, separated by a dot operator (.), e.g., objectName.methodName.

Figure 4-3 shows code that displays an order using the displayOrder method. The line "**newOrder.displayOrder()**" executes the newOrder object's displayOrder method. If we wanted to display a specific Order, we would have included the Order Number as an argument between the method's parentheses, e.g., newOrder.displayOrder(String orderNumber).

```
...
    Order newOrder = new Order( );
    newOrder.displayOrder( );
    ...
```

Figure 4-3: Executing an Object's Method

Inheritance

The process of OOA/D produces numerous classes. Many of these classes are then organized into class hierarchy structures. The top of the hierarchy has characteristics (attributes and behaviors) that are common to all levels below it in the hierarchy. Each level below in a hierarchy is broken into more specific and unique characteristics than the more abstract levels above it, but each of these levels has characteristics that are common to all levels below it.

The Animal kingdom is an example of a class hierarchy. At the top of the hierarchy is the class Animal. The next level down could have the classes Dog, Horse and Pig. Under the class Dog, another level could contain the classes Great Dane, Greyhound and Toy Poodle.

Similar to the Animal class hierarchy, OOA/D classes are also more abstract towards the top of the hierarchy and more specific toward the bottom. If we defined the Animal Class Hierarchy in OOA/D terminology, the class at the top of the class hierarchy is the "superclass." In this case, it would be the Animal superclass. The superclass contains the attributes and behaviors shared by every class below it.

Under the Animal superclass, are the "subclasses" Horse, Dog, and Pig. Under the Dog class are three subclasses, which are Great Dane, Greyhound and Toy Poodle. In this class hierarchy, Dog is a subclass under Animal but a superclass to Great Dane, Greyhound and Toy Poodle. Subclasses inherit the variables and methods from all the classes above it. Figure 4-4 shows this concept.

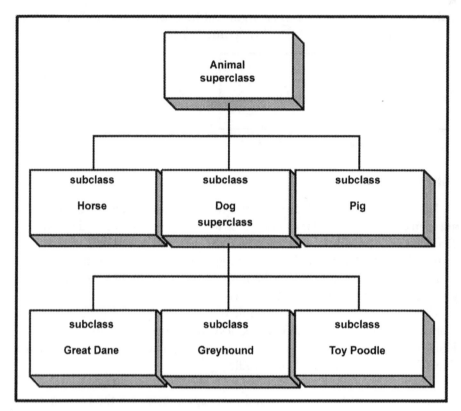

Figure 4-4: Superclasses and Subclasses

Class hierarchies allow development teams to identify reusable Java classes. Developers use the superclasses and subclasses to establish "inheritance" in the code, allowing then to write code once for the common behaviors and variables. A superclass contains common code that subclasses inherit and reuse, reducing the amount of written project code for your Web applications.

Inheritance in an Order Application

We have organized our example Order application into two levels: the superclass, Order, and two subclasses, Purchase Orders for things purchased from outside the company and Work Orders for things built inside the company. The subclasses Purchase Order and Work Order have two variables in common, Order Number and Order Type, and one method in common, Display Order. As shown in Figure 4-5, the common variables and method in the Purchase Order and Work Order classes are used to create the superclass

Order. The subclasses Purchase Orders and Work Orders themselves handle unique requirements for each of these Order Types. For example, a Purchase Order stores the address of where a vendor needs to ship the ordered products.

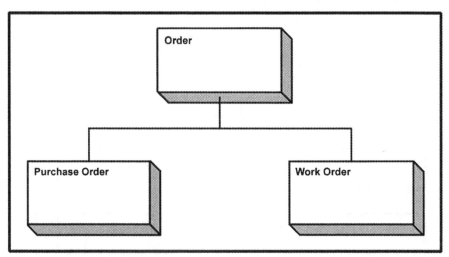

Figure 4-5: Order Class Hierarchy

The UML Class Diagram is used to capture the Order class hierarchy. Figure 4-6 contains a Class Diagram showing the Order class hierarchy. Looking at this Class Diagram, a developer would code the Order class first. Next, the developer would code the Purchase Order and Work Order classes. This allows the subclasses Purchase Order and Work Order to reuse, or inherit, the methods and variables from the Order class. Inheritance can save your team from coding a lot of redundant code.

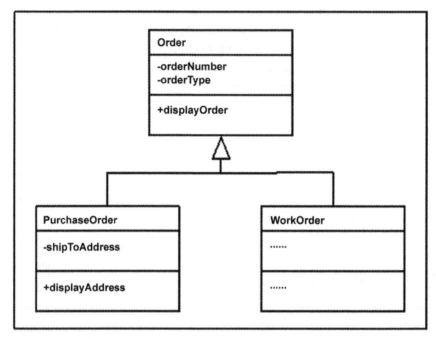

Figure 4-6: Order Class Hierarchy in UML Diagram

Figure 4-7 shows how a developer would code inheritance in the Order system.

o The line "**public class PurchaseOrder extends Order**" defines a new class named PurchaseOrder that extends, or inherits, the variables and methods from the Order class.

```
public class PurchaseOrder extends Order {
    ...
}
```

Figure 4-7: Inheritance Code Created from UML Class Diagram

With inheritance, the PurchaseOrder class has access to the methods and variables in the Order class. This is why inheritance can significantly reduce the amount of code written in any object-oriented project.

Summary

Chapters 3 and 4 presented numerous object-oriented topics including:

o J2EE applications are built primarily using Java, which is an Object-Oriented Programming language (OOP).

o OOP requires Object-Oriented Analysis and Design (OOA/D) techniques like the Unified Modeling Language (UML) to be used during the Requirements and Design phases of a project.

o UML is the industry accepted standard technique for graphically modeling an object-oriented application.

o The UML Class Diagrams depict OOA/D classes and how they relate to each other.

o OOA/D classes are used by developers to define and write their Java application source code.

o All the Java source code written for an application is compiled into Java class files.

o An OOA/D class consists of two components: attributes or data that can be stored about the class and behaviors or operations which can be performed using the attributes.

o Developers convert OOA/D attributes into Java variables.

o Developers convert OOA/D behaviors into Java methods.

o Access modifiers like private and public specify if other Java classes can directly access a class's variables and methods.

o Using the private access modifier for Java variables is known as encapsulation or "data hiding" because the data in a class's private variables are hidden behind the class's public methods.

o An object or instance is created from a class. In Java, the class determines everything that an object does through its methods and stores through its variables.

o Once the object is created, its methods and variables can be accessed.

o To execute an object's method, the code must specify the name of the object and the method to execute, separated by a dot (.) operator.

o The process of OOA/D produces numerous classes and many of these are organized into class hierarchies.

o The top of the class hierarchy is the superclass. The superclass contains the variables and methods shared by every subclass below it.

o Classes under a superclass would be classes called the subclasses of that superclass. Subclasses inherit the variables and methods from all the superclasses above it.

o Developers use the superclasses and subclasses to establish inheritance in their code and allowing then to write code once for the common behaviors and variables.

The remainder of the chapters in this book will discuss the technologies involved in the actual development of J2EE applications.

CHAPTER 5

Development

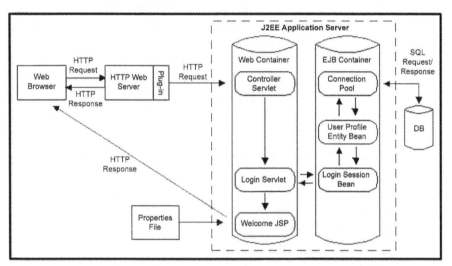

Figure 5-1: Our Example J2EE Application Flow

In the previous chapters, we discussed the importance of having the Requirements and Design efforts produce validated UML documentation that your J2EE developers can use as the basis for creating their application code. The remainder of this book will focus on the components developers use to build J2EE applications. The purpose of these chapters is not to provide an in-depth discussion of the technologies used on J2EE projects, but instead to give a project manager a high-level understanding of how the technologies work together in creating J2EE applications.

We will be using a very simple example application to explain the technical components of developing a J2EE application. We use our example application to illustrate how a HTTP request-response flow would work by logging onto a Web application. We explain this flow, illustrated in Figure 5-1, in more detail throughout the development chapters.

Example Application Flow

Following is an explanation of the flow shown in Figure 5-1. The flow sequence through the example Web application is based on the concept of a HTTP request and HTTP response sequence.

o When a Web browser submits a request for a Web page, it sends a HTTP request to a Web server on the Internet.

o For purposes of this book, we will refer to the Web server as the HTTP Web server because it will be used to service HTTP requests.

o If the HTTP request were for a static Web page, it would be stored in a directory on the HTTP Web server and sent back as a HTTP response from this server. Since our request is for a dynamic Web page, the HTTP Web server will forward the HTTP request to a J2EE application server.

o When the HTTP request is sent to the J2EE application server, the Web container passes this request is to a Java Servlet program called a Controller Servlet.

o The Controller Servlet manages the overall flow and execution of our application on the J2EE application server.

o The Controller Servlet determines the nature of the HTTP request and then forwards the request to the appropriate Business Servlet, in this case, the Login Servlet.

o Each Business Servlet controls the execution of code for a functional area of an application, initiating the execution of required business logic and database access code for that area.

o This business logic and database access code is contained in Enterprise JavaBeans (EJB). Business logic executes as EJB Session Beans, e.g., Login Session Bean.

o As part of its execution process, Session Beans execute any required EJB Entity Beans, e.g., User Profile Entity Beans. Entity Beans read, write, and delete data from a relational database.

o After the Login Session Bean's execution is completed, control returns to the Login Business Servlet that invoked it.

o In our application architecture, the Login Business Servlet then invokes a JavaServer Pages (JSP) called the Welcome JSP.

o This JSP creates the dynamic Web page sent back to the Web browser as a HTTP response.

Technologies in Example Application Flow

J2EE applications can range from very simple in design to extremely complex, depending on the nature of the business problem you are solving. As such, there is not one standard method or process for developing J2EE applications. Therefore, we will not venture to layout a project plan for the development of a J2EE application. Instead, we focus on the different technology components used to develop J2EE applications including:

o   Development languages (Java, HTML, XHTML, XML)

o   J2EE Application Server

o   Relational databases

o   Java Servlets

o   Enterprise JavaBeans (EJB)

o   JavaServer Pages (JSP)

o   Properties files

o   Java APIs

J2EE and Open Standards

J2EE consists of a series of specifications used to define components involved in building, deploying, and managing Java-developed enterprise Web applications. Software vendors use these specifications to create J2EE application servers like IBM's WebSphere® Application Server and by J2EE developers when building Web applications that run on these J2EE application servers. As we pointed out in the previous chapters, a primary benefit of using the Java programming language is the ability to reuse code. J2EE builds upon the concept of code reuse through its support of technology-based open standards and open source code.

In terms of J2EE, open standards are defined by industry standards groups that help ensure that applications developed on one software vendor's J2EE application server will run on any other vendor's J2EE application server. One of the strengths of Java open standards is the availability of reusable open source code known as Java Application Programming Interfaces (API). A Java API is a set of reusable Java code that developers use to avoid starting from scratch each time they write code for an application. Java APIs contain Java classes that have methods and variables that developers use when developing a J2EE application. A developer can use numerous APIs when developing a Web application. For examples, two very popular Java APIs are:

o JDBC API—which provides Java classes that developers use to access relational databases

o JavaMail API—which provides Java classes that developers use to send e-mail

When developers create applications, they can check for available open source Java APIs that will support the building the Web application. Many Java APIs are available from Sun Microsystems® and the Apache Software Foundation®. You can download these APIs from their respective Web sites at no charge. These sites also contain documentation that specifies how to use the API's classes, variables and methods. Using available APIs allow Java developers to concentrate more on writing the application-specific code.

When you download API code from a Web site, it is contained in a single compressed file called a Java archive (JAR) file. JAR files are compressed files similar to ZIP files. JAR files are the Java standard for grouping Java class files into related functions. For example, the Java classes that support access to relational databases are in the JDBC API JAR file. Developers use an "import" directive in their code to use the API JAR files as part of their own application code.

An example of a commonly used JAR file is the Apache Software Foundation's open source log4j API. When creating an application, developers will typically add code to their programs that write status information about what the application is doing at particular moments of execution to a log file. If the application ever fails, developers use the information in the log file to help determine the cause of the failure. Using the log4j API allows developers to reuse proven code that writes entries to the log file without having to create custom logging code themselves.

By helping developers avoid building code commonly used on applications, APIs are essential to increasing developer productivity. As such, researching available Java APIs for possible use in your J2EE application should be included as a task in your project plans.

CHAPTER 6

Static Web Content

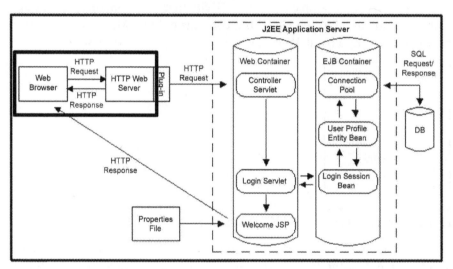

Figure 6-1: Static Web Content

The core technologies used in developing open source J2EE applications include HTML, XML, and Java. Web applications consisting only of static, non-changing pages are written using HTML tags and hard-coded content. The application runs on the HTTP Web server as shown in Figure 6-1.

The information displayed in Dynamic Web applications varies in different situations. These applications combine HTML tags with Java code to generate the dynamic content. Java is the language used to develop the components of a J2EE application server including Java Servlets, Enterprise JavaBeans, and the Java code within the JavaServer pages.

This chapter explains the technologies used specifically to develop static Web applications.

HTML Tags versus Web Page Content

The Hypertext Markup Language (HTML) is a language of pre-defined tags sent by the HTTP Web server with a Web page response to tell the Web browser how to arrange and format the content for the Web page.

It is important to note the difference between Web page content and HTML tags. Web page content is the combination of text, images, video, audio and anything else that displays in the Web browser as part of a Web page. HTML tags arrange the Web page content for display on the page. HTML tags should not display in a Web page (unless there is an error in the HTML code).

Figure 6-2 is an example of an HTML file that only contains HTML tags. Since the code listed in the Figure 6-2 contains only HTML tags and no Web page content, only a blank Web page would display in the Web browser.

```
<html>
    <head>
    </head>
    <body>
        <br/> <br/>
        <b></b>
    </body>
</html>
```

Figure 6-2: HTML Tags to Create Blank Web Page

To have the Web page display something more than a blank page, you need to add content to the HTML file. Figure 6-3 is an example of the previous HTML file with the following Web page content added: "Your Web Page as Plain Text" and "Your Web Page as Bold Text". The code containing <!—HTML tag —> is known as an HTML comment and is not used by the Web browser when it reads the HTML file.

```
<html>                                  <!— HTML tag —>
    <head>                              <!— HTML tag —>
    </head>                             <!— HTML tag —>
    <body>                              <!— HTML tag —>
        Your Web Page as Plain Text        <!— content —>
        <br/><br/>                         <!— HTML tags —>
        <b>Your Web Page as Bold Text</b>  <!— HTML tags and content —>
    </body>                             <!— HTML tag —>
</html>                                 <!— HTML tag —>
```

Figure 6-3: HTML File Containing HTML Tags and Web Page Content

The code listed in the Figure 6-3 produces a Web page that displays the content shown in Figure 6-4 as is appears in a Web browser. This page displays the lines "Your Web Page as Plain Text" in normal font and "Your Web Page as Bold Text" in bold font. The HTML bold tag <b> causes the second line to display in bold text.

Your Web Page as Plain Text
Your Web Page as Bold Text

Figure 6-4: HTML and Content Rendered as Web Page

Figure 6-5 provides another comparison between HTML tags and Web page content. If you are interested in learning more about these and other HTML tags, you can go to the link http://www.w3.org/and click on the HTML link in the left navigation bar. This link takes you to the industry standards pages for HTML.

```
HTML Tags
        <html>
        <head>
        </head>
        <body>
        <br/>
        <br/>
        <b>
        </b>
        </body>
        </html>

Web Page Content
        ◆  Your Web Page as Plain Text
        ◆  Your Web Page as Bold Text
```

Figure 6-5: HTML Tags vs. Web Page Content

Web Page Development Tools

Developers rarely develop Web pages using text editors. Instead, they use Web page design tools like or IBM's WebSphere Studio and Macromedia's Dreamweaver®. These design tools employ a graphical "what-you-see-is-what-you-get" (WYSIWG) visual design to create a Web page's layout. The design tools then generate the HTML tags based upon the design. Web design tools greatly speed the process of designing Web pages and reduce the potential for error in manually coding the Web pages.

Web Page Dummy Content *(Lorem Ipsum)*

When developing the initial design of a Web site's pages, developers do not always know what content to put on each page. To get around this, dummy content text is used.

When reviewing a site during development, users sometimes question the dummy text on a Web page, even if it is clearly dummy text. To avoid this, some developers use dummy content text like "content goes here...content goes here...content goes here..." While it may prevent confusion, this dummy content does not result in a professional design to show users.

A good technique during initial design is to use dummy content text known as *Lorem Ipsum*. Many web page editors can generate *Lorem Ipsum* for dummy text. In addition, there are Web sites available on the Internet that will generate the *Lorem Ipsum* text for you. Figure 6-6 is an example of *Lorem Ipsum* dummy content text.

Lorem ipsum dolor sit amet, consectetuer adipiscing elit. Curabitur imperdiet. In vulputate dui non mi. Morbi at justo. Etiam cursus, purus et volutpat dapibus, enim leo congue urna, vel euismod enim ante nec libero. Phasellus diam massa, nonummy non, iaculis quis, ullamcorper id, nunc. In faucibus neque in neque. Donec feugiat, tortor eu sagittis eleifend, urna urna vulputate sem, ut tincidunt eros ligula non neque. Fusce consectetuer viverra lacus. Fusce sed turpis. Vivamus facilisis sem sit amet felis dictum aliquam. Suspendisse fermentum pede nec massa. Nulla bibendum feugiat nibh. Ut mattis. Cum sociis natoque penatibus et magnis dis parturient montes, nascetur ridiculus mus. Cras a tortor. Sed vitae odio eget justo vulputate faucibus.

Figure 6-6: Lorem Ipsum Dummy Text

Web Page Accessibility

A quality Web site should be accessible for people with disabilities. To do this, you should design your site to support a special Web browser known as a "text reader". These readers convert the textual content of Web pages into speech, allowing the visually-challenged to listen to the Web pages. The readers use keyboard commands, not a mouse, to navigate through a Web the site. For these text readers to work, developers must include additional HTML tags to their Web page code that the readers will understand.

A simple way to test the accessibility of your site's Web pages for people with blindness is to turn off your computer's display monitor and try to navigate the site's pages with a text reader.

Following are two examples of coding a Web page to support these readers: skipping to the main content of a Web page and reading a table on the page.

Skipping to Main Content of Web Page

Many Web sites have a group of links in a navigation bar on the left side or across the top of their Web pages. When a text reader reads a navigational link, it not only reads the name of the link displayed on the Web page, it also reads the URL for the link, which can be quite long in many cases. If a Web site is consistent and puts a left navigational bar on each page, users would have to listen to these navigational links on every page they access. There needs to be a way that allows reader users to skip over the navigation links and start the reader at the main content of Web pages.

A common technique to solve this issue is to have a link at the top of the Web page attached to a hidden image, for example, a spacer image. This link points to the beginning of the Web page's main content, which is usually the Page title. (Figure 6-7) When users display a Web page in the reader, they can immediately display a box of all links contained on the Web page. They can then select the Skip Navigation Bar Links and the reader will begin reading the Web page starting at the Page title.

```
<a href="#skipnavigation">
<img src="images/spacer.gif" width="2" height="2"
     alt="Skip Navigation Links and Go To Main Content"</a>
</a>
...navigation links...
...
<a name="skipnavigation"></a><h1>Web Page Title</h1>
...web page content...
...
```

Figure 6-7: Skipping Left Navigation Links

Reading Table

Web sites use tables to layout tabular data. Tables are similar to spreadsheets in the layout in that they have rows of data and column headers. The text reader needs to be able to read these tables in a way that if a text reader looks in a table cell, it can read the row header and column header to the user.

A common technique to solve this issue is to use the HTML table header tag (TH) to mark the table column and row headers for the table. Figure 6-8 shows an example of coding a table with a person's name and city name to support reading table headers. The <th> tag allows the text reader to speak the column header "Address" and the row header "John Smith" when it reads the cell "316 BookRoad".

```
<table
    <tr>
        <th>Name</th>
        <th>Address</th>
        <th>City</th>
        <th>State</th>
        <th>Zip Code</th>
    </tr>
    <tr>
        <th>John Smith</th>
        <td>316 BookRoad</td>
        <td>Anyplace</td>
        <td>Anystate</td>
        <td>99999</td>
    </tr>
...
</table>
```

Figure 6-8: Reading Table Column and Row Headers

There are many reasons to make a Web site accessible. For example, visually challenged customers may want to purchase products from your commerce site or visually challenged employees may need to use a company's internal web-based Human Resources applications as part of their job responsibilities. Web sites developed for the federal government are required to have accessibility support.

For more information about HTML coding for Web accessibility, go to link http://www.w3.org/and click on the WAI (Web Accessibility Initiative) link in the left navigation bar.

XHTML and XML

The Extensible Hypertext Markup Language (XHTML) is a latest version of HTML standards and will eventually be the standard for writing HTML tag code. XHTML is HTML written to be compliant with Extensible Markup Language (XML) standards.

XML is a very powerful language and is generally used for a variety of purposes on J2EE projects including configuring the J2EE application server and passing data between applications. XML is a major component on projects that include developing Web Services, which allow applications to provide services like business functionality to each other.

Like HTML, XML is a tag language. However, while HTML tags display data on a Web browser, XML tags organize and structure data. Figure 6-9 illustrates this concept.

```
<employee>          <!— XML employee open tag —->
    <name>          <!— XML name open tag —->
        John Smith          <!— name data —->
    </name>         <!— XML name close tag —->
    <city>                  <!— XML city open tag —->
        Atlanta     <!— city data —->
    </city>                 <!— XML city close tag —->
    <phone>         <!— XML phone open tag —->
        999-999-9999        <!— phone data —->
    </phone>        <!— XML phone close tag —->
</employee>         <!— XML employee close tag —->
```

Figure 6-9: XML File Containing Address Data

While HTML tags have meanings that the Web browser understands, XML tags have no meaning except to the application teams developing the XML. In fact, some industry groups and product vendors have standardized XML tags that have particular meaning to their user groups.

XML requires stricter guidelines in its tag syntax than HTML. To accommodate the requirements of XML, XHTML imposes more rigid guidelines on the use of HTML tags than previous versions of HTML.

For example, XHTML has new requirements for HTML tags that were optional in previous HTML versions and XHTML requires all tags to have a closing tag where HTML does not. Based upon this XHTML requirement, every table column tag <td> should have a closing tag </td>.

Figure 6-10 contains a couple additional examples of XHTML compliance requirements for HTML tags.

HTML attribute values must always be quoted, for example, use <td colspan="2"> instead of <td colspan=2>

HTML element and attribute names must be in lower case since XML is case-sensitive, for example, use <table> instead of <TABLE>

Figure 6-10: XHTML Compliance Requirements Examples

If your Web site is required to be XHTML compliant, your developers will need to develop all Web pages to conform to XHTML standards. For more information about XHTML, go to link http://www.w3.org/and click on the XHTML link in the left navigation bar.

CHAPTER 7

J2EE Application Server

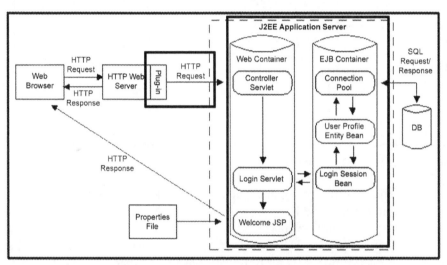

Figure 7-1: J2EE Application Server and HTTP Web Server Plug-In

In our example Web application's architectural design, the HTTP Web server processes any HTTP requests for the application's static Web pages. A Web application's Java code resides and executes on a J2EE application server. When requests are for dynamic Web pages, the J2EE application server creates the pages. The Java code running on this server includes Java Servlets, Enterprise JavaBeans, and JavaServer Pages as identified in Figure 7-1.

Model-View-Controller (MVC) Architecture

We modeled the example Web application flow on a popular J2EE architectural design known as the Model-View-Controller (MVC). In a MVC application design, there are three component areas used to group application code based upon the function that each piece of code performs. Figure 7-2 illustrates this concept.

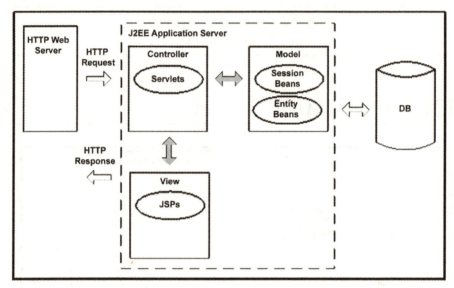

Figure 7-2: Model-View Controller Design

o   The Controller component area handles the incoming HTTP requests
    and controls the flow of the application code based upon the type of
    request. The Controller components consist of the application code
    that receives the HTTP requests and dispatches these requests to the
    Model components for business logic and database access processing.
    When Model processing completes, the Controller initiates a View
    component, which will create a HTTP response that displays on the
    Web browser. The Controller contains the Java Servlet code. (Chapter 9
    discusses Java Servlets.)

o   The Model component area manages both the business logic and the
    interaction with a relational database. The Model components con-
    sist of the application code that stores and accesses the data con-
    tained within a relational database and the business logic that
    operates on this data. For J2EE applications, the Model contains the
    Enterprise JavaBeans code called Entity Beans and Session Beans.
    (Chapter 10 discusses Enterprise JavaBeans.)

o   The View component area generates the Web pages sent back as a
    HTTP response to the Web browser. The View components consist of
    the application code that creates the dynamic Web pages. The View

contains the JavaServer Pages code. (Chapter 11 discusses JavaServer Pages.)

Web and EJB Containers

The J2EE application server is a very complex software program that can do many things, including managing and executing the Java Servlets, JSPs, and EJBs used to generate dynamic Web pages. The J2EE application server uses runtime environments, called containers, to manage and run these Java components of a J2EE application.

Two containers, the Web container and EJB container, execute the Java Servlets, JSPs, and EJBs. Each of these containers has the responsibility of initializing, executing, and destroying the J2EE components deployed within it. As shown in Figure 7-3, the Web container provides these services for the Java Servlet and JSP components and the EJB container provides these services for the EJB components.

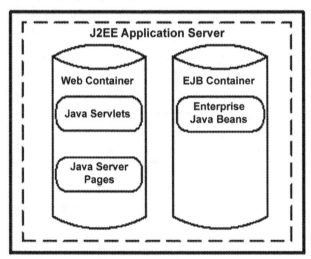

Figure 7-3: Web and EJB Containers

Web Server Plug-In

Static HTML files are stored on the HTTP Web server. When a HTTP request is sent for a static Web page, the HTTP Web server knows how to find this page, which is stored within a directory on the server. Based upon the URL included in the HTTP request, the server looks for the requested Web page in its file directory system and, if found, sends the Web page back to the Web browser as a HTTP response.

In the case of dynamic Web pages, the HTTP Web server forwards the HTTP request to the J2EE application server for processing. This requires the integration of the HTTP Web server and J2EE application server.

A mechanism called a plug-in integrates the HTTP Web server and the J2EE application server. The plug-in configuration determines if a HTTP request is for a dynamic Web page, and if it is, to route the request to J2EE application server.

Figure 7-4 shows a plug-in configuration that routes JSP files to the J2EE application server for processing. The plug-in configuration file is an XML file. J2EE application servers typically generate this XML plug-in file for the HTTP Web server.

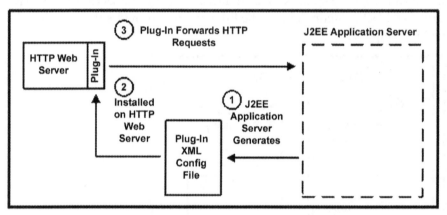

Figure 7-4: HTTP Web Server Plug-In

1. The J2EE application server generates the plug-in XML configuration file for the target HTTP Web server.

2. The team installs the XML configured plug-in onto the HTTP Web server.

3. The HTTP Web server can now determine if a HTTP request is for our Controller Servlet, and if so, forward the request to the J2EE application server.

CHAPTER 8

Dynamic Web Content

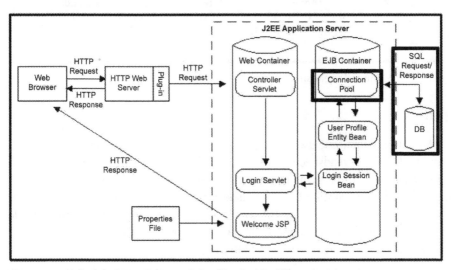

Figure 8-1: Relational Database and Connection Pooling

Dynamic web pages need to interact with databases to get their dynamic web content. (Figure 8-1) This content is typically stored in relational databases like IBM's DB2® and Oracle®, which are the most common databases used by companies to store their enterprise data. Therefore, when creating dynamic Web pages J2EE developers write their code to interact with relational databases. Understanding dynamic Web pages, then, requires a basic knowledge of how relational databases work and the language used by developers to interact with the database.

Relational Database

Relational databases store data in a manner similar to simple spreadsheets. As shown in Figure 8-2, a spreadsheet's design consists of a grid containing

rows and columns. The spreadsheet in Figure 8-2 contains contact information. The columns represent the type of data that is stored in the spreadsheet
like "Name," "Address," and "City". The rows represent the data that is stored
about contacts. Each row represents an individual contact like "John Smith"
and "Mary Jones". A row is equivalent to a record, so a row containing information about John Smith is also a record of information about John Smith.

| Contacts | | | | |
A	B	C	D	E
Name	Address	City	State	Zip code
John Smith	316 BookRoad	Anyplace	Anystate	99999
Mary Jones	678 Chap Place	Anyplace	Anystate	99999

Figure 8-2: Contact Spreadsheet

Tables

A relational database uses a collection of tables to store its data. The design of
these tables, like spreadsheets, consists of a grid containing rows and columns. A
typical database contains many tables. Unique names like "Contacts" or "Orders"
identify each table. Similar to a spreadsheet, records are stored in table rows with
the appropriate data entered in the correct column. Figure 8-3 shows an example
of our "Contacts" as a database table with two rows (one for each person) and
five columns (Name, Address, City, State, and Zip Code).

Name	Address	City	State	Zip Code
John Smith	316 BookRoad	Any place	Any state	99999
Mary Jones	678 Chap Place	Any place	Any state	99999

Figure 8-3: Contacts Table

Structured Query Language

To work with data in a relational database, developers use a standardized
language, the Structured Query Language (SQL). There are three basic things
involved in working with a relational database: creating the tables, granting
access privileges to the tables, and writing data manipulations statements that
interact with the data in the tables.

The first thing a developer needs is to have the relational database tables created. SQL contains a group of commands, known as Data Definition Language (DDL), which are used by developers and database administrators to create, modify (known as alter), and delete (known as drop) tables. Figure 8-4 shows a simplified example of using SQL DDL statements to create the Contacts table.

```
CREATE TABLE CONTACTS

    (NAME          CHAR(25),
    ADDRESS        CHAR(25),
    CITY           CHAR(25),
    STATE          CHAR(25),
    ZIP CODE       CHAR(10)) ;
```

Figure 8-4: Create Contacts Table

Next, a developer needs to have permissions granted in able to access the created tables. SQL has a group of commands, known as the Data Control Language (DCL), used by developers and database administrators to grant, deny and revoke access permissions for each table. Figure 8-5 shows an example of using SQL DCL statements to allow a group of users called JAVA_DEVELOPERS to insert or add data to the Contacts table.

```
GRANT INSERT
    ON CONTACTS
    TO JAVA_DEVELOPERS ;
```

Figure 8-5: Grant Permissions to Contacts Table

With the tables created and permissions granted, the developers can start writing SQL statements that manipulate data within the database. SQL has a group of commands, known as Data Manipulation Language (DML), used by developers and database administrators to insert, read (known as select), update, and delete data from a database. Figure 8-6 shows a simplified example of using SQL DML statements to select all the Names from the Contacts table. Since there are only two rows in our example Contacts table, the result set contains only two rows of Names.

```
The SQL query:
        SELECT NAME FROM CONTACTS ;

Returns the following result set of the two rows:
        NAME
        John Smith
        Mary Jones
```

Figure 8-6: Select Names from Contacts Table

Java Database Connectivity (JDBC) API

Relational database tables store data and developers use the SQL language to access that data. Developers need a way to establish a connection between their Java code and the Web application's relational databases, and to send SQL requests to and receive SQL responses back from the databases.

Java has a standard open source API, called the Java Database Connectivity (JDBC) API, for working with relational databases. The JDBC API provides a set of Java classes that help establish connections with relational databases, sending SQL requests, and receiving SQL responses. For example, before sending a request to the database, a Java application uses the JDBC API classes to connect to the database.

Most database systems, however, have a limited number of connections that can be active at any one time. To get around this in the J2EE architecture, when the J2EE application server opens a database connection, the connection remains active until the database processes the SQL request. After the SQL request is completed, the connection closes or "drops" so other SQL requests can use the connection. Dropping the connection makes it available for other SQL requests to use.

A good example is a Web application that requires a user ID and password for access and stores the IDs and passwords in a database. When a user logs onto the Web application, a connection occurs with the database to retrieve the stored ID/password. After retrieving the stored ID/password, the Java program closes the database connection, freeing it for use by other SQL requests. The application can now validate the user entered ID/password against the stored ID/password.

Connection Pooling

Connecting to a database is an "expensive" process in terms of response times. In fact, some requests for data can take longer to connect to a database than it does to perform the SQL request operation of retrieving the data. To improve the speed of connecting to the database, J2EE applications use the concept of connection pooling. Pooling allows for the sharing of resources. With connection pooling, the application opens a group, or pool, of database connections on the J2EE application server allowing all of the application's SQL requests to share and reuse these connections.

Put simply, when a Java application submits a SQL request, it receives a database connection from the pool as shown in Figure 8-7. When the SQL response returns, the J2EE application server does not drop the database connection. Instead, it returns the connection back to the connection pool. This eliminates the time and resource expense of establishing database connections for each database request.

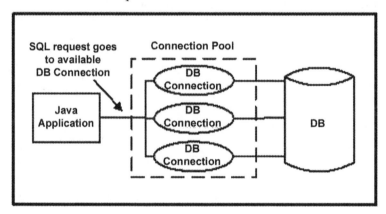

Figure 8-7: Database Connection Pool

Since the J2EE application server manages connection pooling, we can use XML to configure the connection pools. Figure 8-8 is an example of the XML code used to configure the connection pools.

The code specifies the minimum and maximum number of connections that may be in the connection pool at any one time.

The minimum is the number of database connections the application has available when the application first starts up. In the example, the minimum connections allocated for the application is one (1).

The maximum is the number of connections that an application can dynamically grow to if needed. In the example, the maximum limit of connections allocated for the application is ten (10).

Setting a maximum number of connections allows the connection pool to grow from the initial minimum number to meet database connection demand. The reason for specifying minimum and maximum connections is that the more connections there are in the connection pool, the more system resources are used. So the minimum connection number will utilize the least amount of system resources while the maximum connection number will use maximum amount of resources.

```
...
<minimum-pool-size>1</minimum-pool-size>
<maximum-pool-size>10</maximum-pool-size>
...
```

Figure 8-8: Configuring an Application Connection Pool using XML

CHAPTER 9

Java Servlets

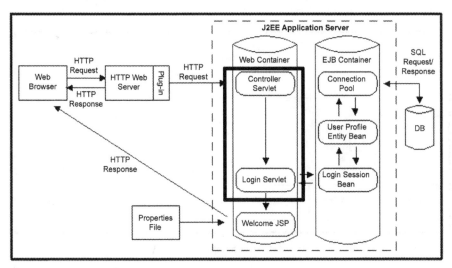

Figure 9-1: Java Servlets

Java Servlets are the primary J2EE technology used to write Java programs that run on a J2EE application server. Figure 9-1 identifies the Java Servlets component area in our Web application model.

Servlet Role in Model-View-Controller

In the Model-View Controller architectural design discussed in Chapter 5, Java Servlets receive HTTP requests for dynamic Web pages from the HTTP Web server and coordinate the development of the HTTP responses returned to the Web browsers. In the MVC design, Servlets control the execution of Enterprise JavaBeans (EJB) and JavaServer Pages (JSP)*. For example, in our

---

* See Chapter 10 for more information about Enterprise Java Beans and Chapter 11 for details on JavaServer Pages.

Web application design, when a HTTP request is sent to the J2EE application server, the server forwards the request to a Java Servlet called a Controller Servlet. This Servlet manages the overall flow of the application.

J2EE applications tend to be large, so the Controller Servlet does not usually execute the Enterprise JavaBeans and JavaServer Pages itself. Instead, the Controller Servlet will execute other Java Servlets known as Business Area Servlets. These Business Area Servlets manage the execution of the Enterprise JavaBeans and JavaServer Pages. As illustrated in Figure 9-2, when a HTTP request comes in, the Controller Servlet determines the nature of the request and then forwards the request to the appropriate Business Area Servlet, which controls the execution of the EJBs.

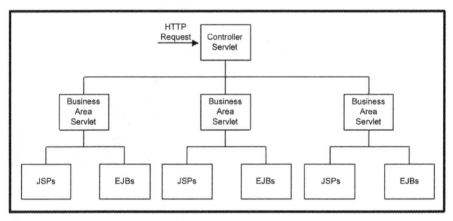

Figure 9-2: Controller and Business Area Servlets

J2EE Servlet Standard Specification

Developers write Java Servlets to comply with the requirements of the J2EE Servlet standard specification. This standard defines how Java Servlets run in the Web container and specifies a set of API classes and methods that any Servlet must implement in order to be able to run in the Web container.

For example, Java Servlet API classes and methods are involved in the creation through deletion lifecycle of a Servlet. The Web container uses these API classes and methods to initialize Servlets that run in the Web container, execute the Servlets to service HTTP requests, and then delete the Servlets when they are no longer needed.

J2EE developers employ Servlet API classes and methods to develop the application's Java Servlets. To use the Servlet API code in their Java programs, developers import the Java API classes into their programs by adding an import directive to their code. (Figure 9-3)

The import directive tells the Java program where to look for an API's class files. The word "directive" is used instead of the word "statement" because Java statements only occur within a class definition, that is, between the class's starting and ending parentheses. The import directive makes reusable code available for Java developers to use in their programs.

- o The directive "**import javax.servlet.***" contains the Servlet API classes used for defining life-cycle methods, among many other things.

- o The directive "**import javax.servlet.http.***" contains the Servlet API classes specifically used for working with HTTP requests and responses

```
import javax.servlet.*;
import javax.servlet.http.*;
public class ControllerServlet extends HttpServlet
{
        // ControllerServlet code goes here
}
```

Figure 9-3: Importing Java Servlet API classes

Java Servlet Used to Generate HTML

Java Servlets existed as part of the J2EE standard before the EJB and JSP specifications were developed. While most developers prefer to use JSPs for generating Web pages, Java Servlets can still be used to can contain both business and database access code (which is the function of EJBs in the Model-View-Controller design) and can generate Web pages (which is the function of JSPs in the Model-View-Controller design). For example, if instead of using a JSP, a Java Servlet generates a Web page, the Servlet generates the HTML tags and Web page content.

- o The Web browser sends a HTTP request to display a Servlet-generated HTML page.

- o The request goes to a HTTP Web server, which forwards the request to the Web container on the J2EE application server.

- o The Web container executes the Servlet with the Java code needed to create the Web page.

o If required, the Servlet reads any data needed from the database and then generates the Web page's HTML tags and content.

o The HTTP response is sent to the Web browser and displays as a Web page.

Figure 9-4 contains a snippet of Java Servlet code used to generate HTML tags and content. As the code illustrates, building a Web page using Servlets requires writing and modifying many lines of Java println statements, which are used to print a line of text from a Java program. Creating the required design of a Web page within a Servlet and then changing the design later can be a very time consuming task and the amount of HTML code within a Servlet makes the Servlet much more difficult to maintain.

```
out.println ("<html>");
out.println ("<head>");
out.println ("</head>");
out.println ("<body>");
out.println ("Your Web Page as Plain Text");
out.println ("<b>Your Web Page as Bold Text</b>");
out.println ("</body>");
out.println ("</html>");
```

Figure 9-4: Servlet Code to Write Out HTML Tags

Session Management

When the J2EE application server receives a HTTP request and then sends a HTTP response, the server forgets anything that it did with the request and response. The next time the same Web browser sends a HTTP request, the server does not recall anything about the previous HTTP request.

For example, in an online shopping cart, each step involved in adding three items to a shopping cart, checking out and paying would need to be done in a single HTTP request because the J2EE application server would not be able to remember anything beyond that single request. This means that adding three books to the shopping cart and clicking a checkout button could take four or more HTTP requests.

The Web container provides the Java Servlet a relatively simple solution, Session management, for handling the shopping cart scenario. Session management uses an object called HttpSession to retain information between the HTTP requests. The HttpSession or Session object is created for a particular HTTP request and then persists for the entire sequence of HTTP requests from that particular Web browser so that any request can use the retained information. The length of time the information is stored on the J2EE application server is configurable and is typically determined by the application need.

In Figure 9-5, Web browser # 111 sends a HTTP request to the J2EE application server. The first time the server receives this request, the Java Servlet creates the Session object for # 111 and stores needed information in the Session object. On subsequent HTTP requests from Web browser # 111, the Java Servlet reads the information stored in the Session object and stores new information in the Session object. The coding examples later in this chapter further explain this concept.

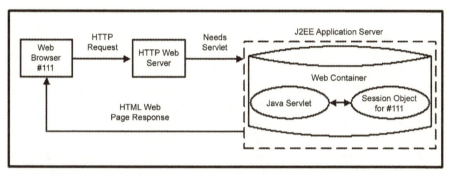

Figure 9-5: Session Object

The line of code in Figure 9-6 creates a Session object. This code returns the current Session object associated with the HTTP request or, if the request does not have one, creates a new Session object. If the getRequest attribute has the value of false instead of true, the getSession method returns only the existing Session object and no new Session object will be created.

```
HttpSession session = request.getSession(true);     // create the session object
```

Figure 9-6: Creating a Session Object

When the Web container creates the Session object, it creates a Session ID, which uniquely identifies the Session object within the Web container. The Session ID is included each time the HTTP response is sent to the Web browser, typically in a Web browser cookie. The Web browser sends the information in the cookie, including the Session ID, each time an additional HTTP request for an application is sent to the J2EE application server.

The Web container uses this Session ID to associate an existing Session object with the incoming HTTP request. The Session object and Session ID allow previous HTTP request session information to be used with any new HTTP request.[*]

The setAttribute and getAttribute methods in Figure 9-7 are used to write data to the Session object and then read data from it. The setAttribute method stores an attribute and its associated value into the Session object. The getAttribute reads the attribute and its value from the Session object.

```
session.setAttribute(attribute_name, attribute_value);  // write attribute to session object
session.getAttribute(attribute_name);                   // read attribute from session object
```

Figure 9-7: Working with the Session Object

For security reasons, the Session object should be deleted when it is no longer needed. Developers use the Session object's "invalidate" method in their Java Servlet code to delete the Session object. This approach is typically used when a user clicks the Sign out or Log off button on a Web page. However, if the user just closes the Web browser instead of clicking on the Sign out button, the Session object stays active in the Web container. This opens the possibility that a hacker could break into the Web application and access the user's bank account.

To help solve this security issue, a second technique is employed in J2EE applications to delete the Session object. This technique consists of telling the Web container how much time a Session object can be inactive before it is deleted from the container. For example, an online banking application may only allow 10 minutes of inactivity between HTTP requests.

Figure 9-8 shows the XML used to configure the Web container to time out our example application's Session objects after 10 minutes of HTTP request inactivity.

```
<session-config>
        <session-timeout>10</session-timeout>
</session-config>
```

Figure 9-8: Configuration Setting to Timeout Session Object

---

[*] If the Web browser has its cookies disabled, there is another technique called URL rewriting that also allows the Session ID to be written to the HTTP responses, causing the subsequent HTTP requests to contain the Session ID. URL rewriting is not discussed in this book.

ControllerServlet Code

Following is an example of how Java Servlets work in the example application.

- o A user visits the Web page containing the HTML code shown in Figure 9-9, which renders the page shown in Figure 9-10. Most of the lines of HTML code shown in Figure 9-9 are contained between opening and closing form tags. The importance of form tags is that they contain the input tag values, which are included as part of the HTTP request when the form is submitted.

- The lines "<form method="post" action="../servlet/ControllerServlet">" and "</form>" are known as form tags. The **method** attribute in the example specifies a post method type, which means that the data the user entered into the form is embedded in the HTTP request. The ControllerServlet uses the type of method sent in the HTTP request to determine which code it will execute. We will see this when the Controller Servlet code is discussed further down. The **action** attribute contains the URL we want executed, in this case, it specifies the name of our Java Servlet called ControllerServlet.

- The line "<input type="text" name="login_userid" size="10"/>" is used to display the User ID text input field on a Web page. The **name** attribute assigns a name to the input field. The ControllerServlet uses the name **login_userid** to access the value entered in the User ID by the user. The **size** attribute specifies the size of the input box field that will display on the Web page.

- The line "<input type="password" name="login_password" size="10"/>" is used to display the Password input field on a Web page. Specifying the input tag type as **password** causes the Password to be obscured with asterisks as it is entered. The ControllerServlet uses the name **login_password** to access the Password value entered by the user.

- The line "<input type="hidden" name="BusinessServlet" value="LoginServlet"/>" is used to specify a hidden field, which means that the field will not be displayed on the Web page. This hidden field specifies a name, **BusinessServlet**, which contains the value of the Business Area Servlet we want the ControllerServlet to execute. In this case, we want the ControllerServlet to execute the **LoginServlet**.

- The line "<input type="submit" value="Submit"/>" specifies a button to display on the Web page. The user clicks this button to submit the form as a HTTP request. The **value** attribute specifies the label that displays on the button.

o The user enters a user ID and password, which is submitted as a HTTP request to log onto the Web application.

```
<html>
Log In to Our Application<br/><br/>
<form method="post" action="../servlet/ControllerServlet">
User ID: <input type="text" name="login_userid" size="10"/><br/>
Password: <input type="password" name="login_password" size="10"/>
<input type="hidden" name="BusinessServlet" value="LoginServlet"/>
<input type="submit" value="Submit"/>
</form>
</html>
```

Figure 9-9: HTML to Submit HTTP Request that Executes Controller Servlet

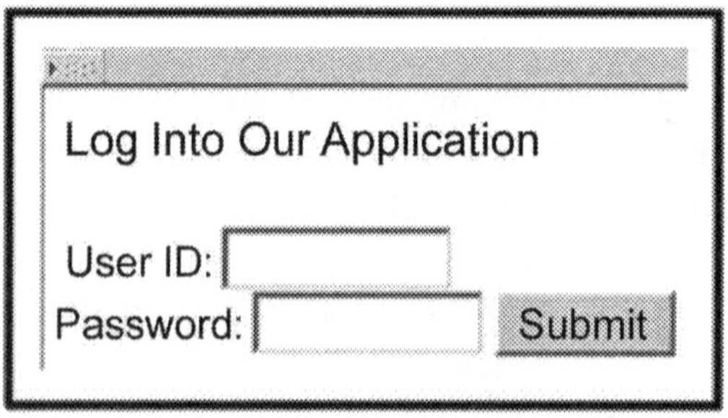

Figure 9-10: HTML Rendered as Web Page

o After the user submits the Login HTTP request, the HTTP Web server receives the request and determines that it is for the ControllerServlet. The HTTP Web server uses the XML configured Web server plug-in to forward the request to the J2EE application server for processing.

o The J2EE application server sends the HTTP request to the Web container, which processes the request by executing the ControllerServlet. When the Web container gets the HTTP request, it creates both a HTTPServletRequest (Request) object and a HTTPServletResponse (Response) object that the ControllerServlet uses to read data from the HTTP request and to write data to the HTTP response. Figure 9-11 illustrates this concept.

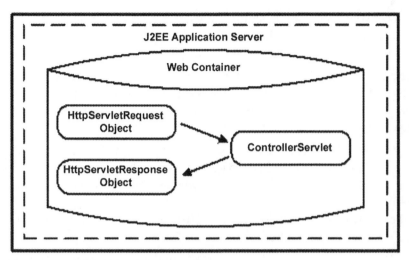

Figure 9-11: HTML Rendered as Web Page

o The ControllerServlet uses the HttpServletRequest object to read the HTTP request, including the parameters passed in the request. It determines that it needs to execute the Business Area Servlet called the Login Servlet. The ControllerServlet then initiates the execution of the LoginServlet. The snippets of code in Figure 9-12 demonstrate how the ControllerServlet executes this process.

```
import javax.servlet.*;
import javax.servlet.http.*;
public class ControllerServlet extends HttpServlet {
    public void doPost(HttpServletRequest request, HttpServletResponse response) {
        HttpSession session = request.getSession(true);
        if ("LoginServlet".equals(request.getParameter ("BusinessServlet") ) ) {
            session.setAttribute("s_userid", request.getParameter("login_userid") );
            session.setAttribute("s_password", request.getParameter("login_password") );
        }
        response.sendRedirect("../servlet/LoginServlet");
    }
}
```

Figure 9-12: ControllerServlet Code

o The Web container executes the code shown in Figure 9-12. The ControllerServlet is the entry point for execution of the HTTP request by our application.

- Through the concept of inheritance, the ControllerServlet extends the class HttpServlet so that it can process HTTP requests and responses. The line "**public class ControllerServlet extends HttpServlet**" creates the ControllerServlet class that extends the HttpServlet class.

- In the HTML code, there was the line "**<form method="post" action="../servlet/ControllerServlet">**", which shows a post method was sent. The HttpServlet class has a method called doPost to handle HTTP requests containing the **post** form value. The line "**public void doPost(HttpServletRequest request, HttpServletResponse response)**" declares the doPost method.

- The Web container sees the post value sent in the HTTP request and executes the doPost method. This method contains two arguments: HttpServletRequest request and HttpServletResponse response. These arguments provide the ControllerServlet access to the HttpServletRequest and HttpServletResponse objects created by the Web container.

- The line "**HttpSession session = request.getSession(true)**" is used to create the Session object that will be used to store information about the interactions between the user Web browser and the processing of the user's HTTP requests on the J2EE application server. Since the setting is true, the next time the user sends the ControllerServlet a HTTP request, the ControllerServlet can use the information in the existing Session object.

- In the HTML code, there was the line "**<input type="hidden" name="BusinessServlet" value="LoginServlet"/>**", which declared hidden field BusinessServlet containing the value LoginServlet. The line "**if ("LoginServlet".equals(request.getParameter ("BusinessServlet")))**" tests if the value passed in the BusinessServlet is equal to the value LoginServlet. In our case, this is true so the code between the brackets will execute. The code **request.getParameter** means that the parameter BusinessServlet is read from the HttpServletRequest Request object.

- In the HTML code, there was the line "**<input type="text" name="login_userid" size="10"/>**" that declared field login_userid containing the User ID value. The line "**session.setAttribute("s_userid", request.getParameter("login_userid"))**" writes the login_userid value read from the HttpServletRequest Request object to the Session object. Its new name in the Session object is s_userid.

- In the HTML code, there was the line "<input type="text" name="login_password" size="10"/>" is which declared field login_password containing the Password value. The line "session.setAttribute("s_password", request.getParameter("login_password"))" writes the login_password value read from the HttpServletRequest Request object to the Session object. Its new name in the Session object is s_password.

- The line "response.sendRedirect("../servlet/LoginServlet")" causes the LoginServlet to execute.

LoginServlet Code

The LoginServlet controls the business process logic for logging into our application. The LoginServlet executes an EJB Login Session Bean method located in the EJB container. This Login Session Bean method compares the Password included in the HTTP request against the Password stored in our application's relational database and passes the result back to the LoginServlet. If the Passwords are equal, the LoginServlet executes the Welcome JSP, which is the home page for any user who successfully logs into our application. The snippets of code in Figure 9-13 shows the LoginServlet code for executing this log in process.

```
import javax.servlet.*;
import javax.servlet.http.*;
public class LoginServlet extends HttpServlet {
    public void doPost(HttpServletRequest request, HttpServletResponse response) {
        HttpSession session = request.getSession(false);
        Object homeObject = jndiContext.lookup("ejb/Login");
        LoginHome loginHome = (LoginHome)
            (javax.rmi.PortableRemoteObject.narrow(homeObject,LoginHome.class));
        Login loginobject = loginHome.create();
        int compareUseridPwd = loginobject.loginUser
            (session.getValue("s_userid").toString(),
             session.getValue("s_password").toString());
        if (compareUseridPwd == 1) {
            response.sendRedirect("../jsp/Welcome.jsp");
        }
    }
}
```

Figure 9-13: LoginServlet Code

The LoginServlet code shown in Figure 9-13 is a Java Servlet like the ControllerServlet and, as such, there is similarity in some of the code such as extending the class HttpServlet, declaring the doPost method, and using the Session object. The code snippet is missing much of the complexity of connecting a Java Servlet residing in the Web container to an EJB Session bean in running in the EJB container. Nevertheless, we left in a couple lines of this complex code to demonstrate the connection between the Java Servlet and EJB Session bean.

- The line "**HttpSession session = request.getSession(false)**" is used to access the Session object created in the ControllerServlet. Now the LoginServlet has access to the User ID and Password passed in the HTTP request and stored in the Session object by the ControllerServlet.

- The lines "**Object homeObject = jndiContext.lookup("ejb/Login");**" "**LoginHome loginHome = (LoginHome) (javax.rmi.PortableRemote Object.narrow(homeObject,LoginHome.class));**" and "**Login loginobject = loginHome.create();**" are part of a larger group of code for connecting the LoginServlet with the Login Session bean. Since the LoginServlet runs in the Web container and the Login Session bean runs in the EJB container, this code finds and provides the LoginServlet a reference or access to the Login Session bean.

- Now that the LoginServlet has reference to the Login Session bean class, it can execute one of its class methods. The line "**int compareLoginIdPwd = loginobject.loginUser(session.getValue ("s_userid").toString() session.getValue("s_password").toString());**" does several things. It reads the User ID and Password sent in the HTTP request and stored in the Session object by the ControllerServlet, and then passes these two values as arguments when it executes the Login session bean's loginUser method. The loginUser method compares the Password sent in the HTTP request and a Password stored in the relational database and returns a "1" if the values are equal. This return value is stored in the Java variable compareLoginIdPwd.

- The line "**if (validIdPwd == 1)**" tests if the value returned from the loginUser method value is equal to "1". In our case, this is true so the code between the brackets will execute.

- The line "**response.sendRedirect("../jsp/Welcome.jsp");**" causes the Welcome.jsp to execute. This JSP welcomes you to our application's home page.

CHAPTER 10

Enterprise Java Beans

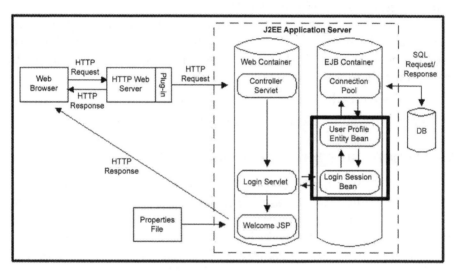

Figure 10-1: Enterprise JavaBeans

Enterprise JavaBeans (EJB) are a standard component-based J2EE technology for writing Java programs that interact with relational databases and execute an application's business logic. Figure 10-1 identifies the EJB component area in our Web application model.

Developers can create three types of EJBs for an application: Entity beans, Session beans, and Message-driven beans. Entity beans send SQL requests to relational databases and Session beans execute an application's business logic. In other words, Entity beans access the data and Session beans use or process the data. In data and process modeling, Entity beans represent things like Orders, Addresses and Users, and are expressed as nouns with names like Order Entity bean, Address Entity bean, and UserProfile Entity bean. Session beans represent processes like Create Order, Update Address, and User Login, and are expressed as verbs with names like CreateOrder Session bean, UpdateAddress Session bean, and Login Session bean.

(Message-driven beans are not as widely used as Entity and Session beans and are not discussed in this book.)

Entity Beans

Entity beans define the Java methods, attributes, and primary keys for accessing data stored within relational databases. J2EE developers typically use Entity beans to handle the sending of SQL requests to the relational databases that store, read, update or delete data.

There are two types of Entity beans: Container-managed persistence (CMP) and Bean-managed persistence (BMP). The primary difference between the types of Entity beans are in the creation of the SQL statements used in the SQL requests to the relational databases.

o   CMP uses the EJB container to generate the SQL statements.

o   BMP requires the developer to write the SQL statements themselves.

Container-Managed Persistence (CMP)

Creating CMP Entity beans is primarily a mapping exercise. Developers create CMP Entity beans by using their Java development tool to map the Entity bean variables to corresponding attributes represented in relational database tables. After mapping the bean variables to the database table attributes, the developers use an integrated Java development tool, like WebSphere Application Studio Director®, to generate the CMP Entity bean code used by the EJB container.

In Figure 10-2, the Customer Entity bean maps to the Customer table, the Order Entity bean maps to the Order table, and the OrderItem Entity bean maps to the Order Item table. When the Order Entity bean executes, the SQL statements generated by the EJB container is sent as a SQL request to the Order table.

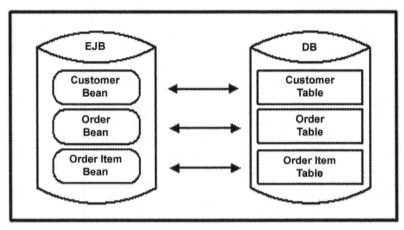

Figure 10-2: Container Managed Persistence Mapping

Bean-Managed Persistence (BMP)

With BMP Entity beans, developers write the actual Java and SQL request statements needed to add, read, update, or delete data in a database table. The flow of SQL requests and responses between BMP Entity beans and a database is essentially the same as for CMP Entity beans.

To understand the difference between CMP and BMP Entity beans, think about how each Entity bean type would read data from two related tables. For example, let's say we are developing an Order application and one of the application's Web pages needs to display an Order record and its associated Order Line Item records. If CMP beans were used in to develop the Entity beans, two CMP Entity beans would need to be created:

o   An Order Entity bean to read the Order table

o   An OrderItem Entity bean to read the Order Item table

You would need to execute both the Order and OrderItem Entity beans to read the records from both these tables.

If BMP were used in developing the application, one Order Entity bean could read both the Order and Order Item tables. Figure 10-3 illustrates this concept.

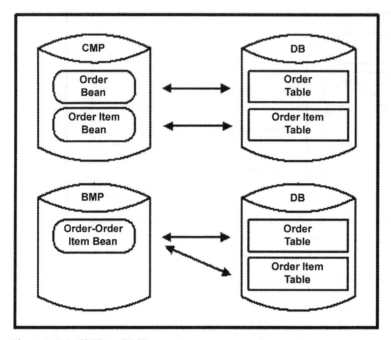

Figure 10-3: CMP vs. BMP

It is important to understand that the type of EJB used in an application requires different development processes for CMP and BMP Entity beans. Each Entity bean type has its advantages and disadvantages, and your application architect will determine which type to use on your project based upon the requirements for the application. For the J2EE developer, BMP beans mean a greater programming effort, so if BMP beans are used; this additional amount of coding will have a direct impact on development time and should be included in time estimates.

Session Beans

While Entity beans handle the interaction with the database, Session beans execute business process logic like placing an order or verifying a credit card. Session beans invoke Entity beans when access to a database is required. In Figure 10-4, the Order Session bean manages the process of creating an Order. The Order Session bean executes the Order Entity bean to retrieve or store data about an Order.

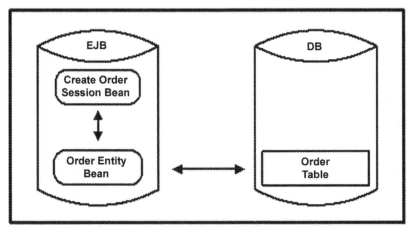

Figure 10-4: Session and Entity beans

There are two types of Session beans: Stateless or Stateful.

When Stateful Session beans are used, each user created by the initial Web browser HTTP request is given his or her own copy of the Session bean. The Stateful Session bean stays associated to the user throughout the many interactions between the user's HTTP requests and the server's responses until the user closes the Web browser or the session times out. This persistence allows the Session bean itself to remember details about previous interactions between the HTTP requests and the J2EE application server.

On the other hand, with Stateless Session beans, HTTP requests share a common copy of Session beans. Unlike the Stateful Session bean, Stateless Session beans do not persist beyond the one HTTP request and HTTP response cycle. Stateless Session beans are the more commonly used Session bean on projects due to improved performance of sharing beans among users versus dedicating beans to each user.

Your application architect determines whether a Session bean should be Stateful or Stateless. While these decisions are not of much importance to a project manager, the type of Session bean used has an impact on the J2EE application server's performance and scalability.

J2EE EJB Standard Specification

Developers write EJBs to comply with the requirements of the J2EE Enterprise JavaBeans standard specification. Similar to using the Servlet standard, developers utilize EJB API classes to develop their application's EJBs. To use EJB API class code in their Java programs, developers import these classes into their programs by using the following line of code. Figure 10-5 shows this code.

- The directive **"import javax.ejb.*"** is used to import the EJB API classes.

```
import javax.ejb*;
public class LoginBean implements SessionBean {
        //LoginBean code goes here
}
```

Figure 10-5: Importing EJB API classes into Session bean

Login Session Bean Code

The Login Session bean's role is to compare the Password entered by the user and sent in the HTTP request against the user's Password stored in the User Profile relational database table. When the comparison is complete, it returns a value back to the LoginServlet which indicates if the Passwords where equal or not. Figure 10-6 shows the code for a Login Session bean.

```
import javax.ejb.*;
public class LoginBean implements SessionBean {
    public int loginUser(String enteredUserid, String enteredPassword) {
        Object homeObject = jndiContext.lookup
            (mySessionCtx.getEnvironment().getProperty("LOOKUP_NAME_
            USERPROFILE"));
        UserProfileHome userobject = (UserProfileHome)
            (javax.rmi.PortableRemoteObject.narrow(homeObject,UserProfileHome.
            class));
        UserProfile userProfile = userobject.findByKey(enteredUserid);
        if (enteredPassword.equals(userProfile.getPassword())) {
            return 1;        // passwords are the same
        else
            return 2;        // passwords are different
        }
    }
}
```

Figure 10-6: Login Session bean code

Figure 10-6 shows a snippet of the code executed by the EJB container. The code shown here compares the Passwords and returns the result of this comparison to the LoginServlet.

o The line "**public class LoginBean implements SessionBean**" creates the LoginBean Session bean class. LoginBean implements the SessionBean interface, a different type of Java class. Every Session bean created for an application must implement this interface since the EJB container uses its methods to manage Session beans.

o The LoginServlet code contained the line "**int compareLoginIdPwd = loginobject.loginUser(session.getValue("s_userid").toString() session. getValue("s_password").toString());**" that executes the Login Session bean method called loginUser. This method is contained in the Session bean class named LoginBean. The line "**public int loginUser(String enteredUserid, String enteredPassword)**" declares the loginUser method receives two values, the User ID and Password sent in the HTTP request. In addition, the 'int' means that when this method completes executing, it will return an integer value like 1 or 2.

o The lines "**Object homeObject = jndiContext.lookup (mySessionCtx.getEnvironment().getProperty("LOOKUP_NAME_ USERPROFILE"));**" and "**UserProfileHome userobject = (UserProfileHome) (javax.rmi.PortableRemoteObject.narrow(home Object,UserProfileHome.class));**" are part of a larger group of code for connecting the LoginBean with the UserProfile Entity bean. This code finds the Use Profile Entity bean in the EJB container and then provides the LoginBean a reference or access to it.

o Now that the LoginBean has reference to the UserProfile Entity bean class, it can execute the FindByKey method. This method finds the User Profile record in the relational database based upon the User ID. The line "**UserProfile userProfile = userobject.findByKey (enteredUserid);**" uses the User ID passed to the loginUser method to find the User Profile record..

o The line "**if (enteredPassword.equals(userProfile.getPassword()))**" tests if the Password passed to the loginUser method is equal to Password read from the User Profile table. If the comparison is true, the line "**return 1;**" will execute and return the value '1' to the LoginServlet. If the comparison is false, the line "**return 2;**" will execute and return the value '2' to the LoginServlet.

UserProfile Entity Bean Code

The UserProfile Entity bean's role is to read the Password stored in the User Profile relational database table and return it to the Login Session bean. Figure 10-7 shows the code for doing this. For CMP Entity beans, the below code is generated for the previously discussed mapping exercise.

```
public class UserProfileBean implements EntityBean {
        public getPassword() {
                return password;
        }
}
```

Figure 10-7: UserProfile Entity bean code

The EJB container executes the code shown in Figure 10-7.

o   The line "**public class UserProfileBean implements EntityBean**" creates the UserProfileBean class.

o   In the LoginBean code, there was the line "**if (enteredPassword. equals(userProfile.getPassword()))**" which executed the Login Session Bean method called loginUser. The line "**public getPassword()**" returns the stored Password to the LoginBean and is used in the if statement that compares the two passwords.

CHAPTER 11

JavaServer Pages

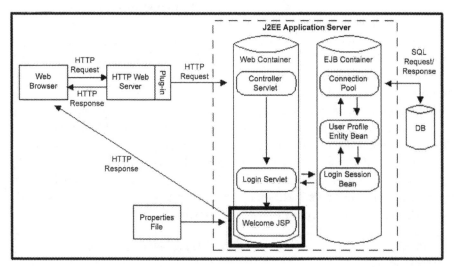

Figure 11-1: JavaServer Pages

Chapter 9 demonstrated how to use JavaServlets to create the HTML for dynamic Web pages. This chapter explains how to use another J2EE technology, JavaServer Pages (JSP), to create the same dynamic Web pages. Figure 11-1 identifies the JSP technology area in our Web application model.

JSPs versus Java Servlets

Although Java Servlets can generate the HTML tags used to build dynamic Web pages, JSPs are the preferred J2EE technology for this task.

This is because there are many differences between using a Java Servlet to generate a Web page versus using a JSP to generate the page. One of these is the approach used to create the code for the Web page:

o With Java Servlets, the developer writes the Java code first and then later inserts the HTML code into the Java code.

o With JSPs, the developer writes the HTML code first and then later inserts the Java code into the HTML code.

Using the JSP approach as opposed to Java Servlets allows the developer to design and display an application's Web pages first using HTML tags and static content. This allows the development team to validate and modify the Web page designs before undertaking the more complex Java development within the JSPs. After the user community approves the Web page designs, developers replace the appropriate static content with Java code to create the dynamic content for the Web pages.

Another advantage of using the JSP approach is that the project team can build the Web pages in HTML using WYSIWYG Web page designers, freeing the Java developers to focus on other activities like the object-oriented design and programming tasks.

Figure 11-2 shows an example of replacing static content with dynamic content within a JSP file. To include Java code within the HTML code, the developer would insert the code within a scriptlet, placing the code between the scriptlet's <%...%> tags, i.e., <%= **titletable.getAttribute("title_as_text")** %>. The Java code that creates the dynamic content is contained between "<%" and "%>" JSP tags. (Although not shown here, these lines of dynamic code require additional lines of Java code to work.)

Web Page Developed with Static Content	Web Page Developed with Dynamic Content
<html>	<html>
<head>	<head>
</head>	</head>
<body>	<body>
Your Web Page as Plain Text	<%= titletable.getAttribute("title_as_text") %>
Your Web Page as Bold Text	<%= titletable.getAttribute("title_as_bold") %>
</body>	</body>
</html>	</html>

Figure 11-2: Static Content versus JSP

JSPs versus HTML Files

Modifying static Web page content requires changing the HTML files themselves. However, with JSP files, Web page content is stored in a relational database, allowing the content to change without modifying the JSP files. This is because the Java variables read these values from the relational database every time the JSP executes. Figure 11-3 illustrates this concept.

o To change static content in a HTML file, a developer modifies, tests and saves the file as a new version of the code. The developer then deploys the file in a directory on the HTTP Web server, overriding the previous version of the code. After deploying the file, the HTTP Web server sends the new HTML file to Web browsers requesting the Web page.

o To change dynamic content in a JSP file, any authorized business user or project team member can change the data in a relational database. The next time a Web browser requests the JSP, the dynamic Web page displays with the new content. Using a JSP to read its content from a relational database eliminates the need to modify and re-deploy the JSP on its J2EE application server to change content for a Web page.

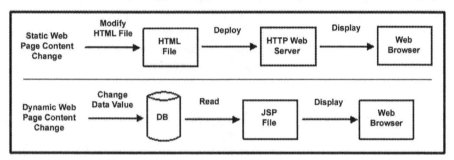

Figure 11-3: Changing Static and Dynamic Web Page Content

J2EE JSP Standard Specification

Developers write JSPs to comply with the requirements of the J2EE JavaServer Pages standard specification. Similar to using Java Servlet standard API classes, developers utilize the JSP API classes to develop their application's JSPs. To utilize the JSP API class code in their Java programs, developers import the classes into their programs by using the lines of code shown in Figure 11-4.

o The directives "**import javax.servlet.***" and "**import javax.servlet.jsp.***" are used to import the JSP API classes.

```
<%@ page import="javax.servlet.* %>

<%@ page import="javax.servlet.jsp %>
        ...
        ...
        //html and java statements
        ...
        ...
```

Figure 11-4: Importing JSP API class code

You may have noticed that the use of the word "servlet" in the import directives for JSPs. The reason for this is that the Web container treats JSPs as if they were Java Servlets. When a JSP deploys into the Web container, the container changes the JSP into Java source code and compiles the Java code into a Java Servlet class file. Then the Web container runs the JSP like it executes any other Java Servlet.

JSP Similarity to Java Servlet Execution

The execution of a HTTP request using a JSP is very similar to executing a request using a Java Servlet. The Web browser sends the HTTP request to the HTTP Web server, which forwards the request to the J2EE application server. The J2EE application server finds and executes the JSP code. Instead of generating the HTML tags like Servlets, the JSP file merges the dynamic content generated from the JSP Java code with the JSP's static HTML tags. The J2EE application server then sends the dynamically generated Web page back as a HTTP response to the requesting Web browser, which displays the Web page.

JSP Standard Tag Library (JSTL)

JSP technology has been evolving and it is now possible to develop JSP pages using tag libraries instead of Java code contained within scriptlets. Developing with tag libraries is similar to using languages like Javascript and XML, allowing non-Java developers to create and maintain JSP pages.

To use tag libraries in an application's JSPs, developers employ the JSP Standard Tag Library (JSTL), which provides a set of reusable standard tag libraries for creating dynamic JSP pages. For the JSP developer, these tag libraries are not as powerful as the Java language because they cannot do everything that Java code can do. However, tag libraries provide much of the functionality needed to develop dynamic JSP pages for a Web site.

In Figure 11-5, the <c:out value=.../> tag will display the text contained in the value attribute, for example, <c:out value="${title_as_text}"/> displays as "Your Web Page as Plain Text" and <c:out value="${title_as_bold}"/> displays as "Your Web Page as Bold Text". Similar to our other code examples, these two JSTL tags need additional lines of code for them to work.

Web Page Developed with Scriptlets	Web Page Developed with JSTL

``html
<html>
 <head>
 </head>
 <body>
  <%= titletable.getAttribute("title_as_text") %>
  <b><%= titletable.getAttribute("title_as_bold") %></b>
 </body>
</html>
``
	``html
	<html>
	 <head>
	 </head>
	 <body>
	  <c:out value="${title_as_text}" />
	  <b><c:out value="${title_as_bold}" /></b>
	 </body>
	</html>
	``

Figure 11-5: Scriptlets versus JSTL tags

CHAPTER 12

Properties Files Content

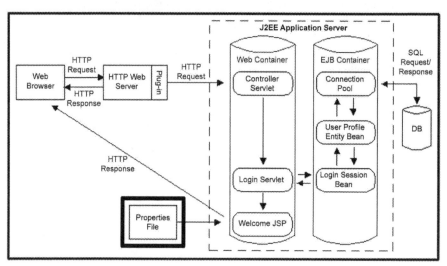

Figure 12-1: Properties File

J2EE applications typically read dynamically generated Web page content from relational databases. However, some Web page content can come from a source different than a relational database. For example, content can come from a text-based file, the Properties file, which is stored on the J2EE application server. Figure 12-1 shows where the Properties file fits into our example application.

Static Content on Dynamic Pages

Certain types of Web page content are relatively static and do not necessarily benefit from being stored in a relational database. For example, a Web page that prompts users to enter their street mailing address has field labels like "Name" and "Address". These field labels, as shown in Figure 12-2, tell the users what type of data to enter into each input field. Web page field labels typically do not change frequently.

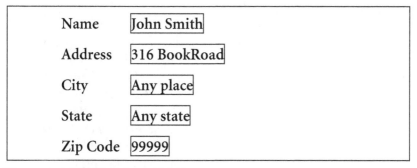

Figure 12-2: Field Labels on Web Page

Hard-Coded Field Labels

One option for getting the field labels to appear on Web pages is to hard-code the field labels into the actual JSP files. However, modifying hard-coded field labels can cause problems when the labels do change. Changing hard-coded labels requires that the JSP developers edit the JSP files. This introduces a larger potential for error since editing code carries with it the risk of breaking the code. Additionally, if the modified field labels exist on more than one Web page for the Web application, each affected JSP file needs to be changed.

An example of a business requirement to change field labels might be a Web application originally developed to support users in the United States but that now needs to support Canadian users. The new business requirement would include changing the street address Zip Code field label from "Zip Code" to "Zip/Postal Code."

As shown in Figure 12-3, hard-coded input labels require developers to identify and modify each JSP that displays the Zip Code field label. On large Web applications, this is not as simple a task as it may sound because every modified JSP needs testing to ensure nothing was broken while the JSP developer was modifying the code.

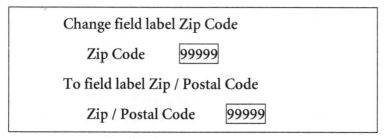

Figure 12-3: Modifying Field Labels on Web Pages

Properties Files Field Labels

Instead of hard-coding static content, Java offers a simple alternative that allows textual content to be stored the in a text file and then to use a Java API to read the file. This text file is known as a Properties file. In Figure 12-3, the field label for Zip Code is stored in a Properties file. The JSP developer would change the "Zip Code" label in the Properties file to "Zip Code/Postal Code." Since the developer had originally coded the JSP to access the field labels in the Properties files, the modified label "Zip Code/Postal Code" will begin appearing on the Web pages without modifications to any of the JSP files.

Properties Files Structure

The Properties files use a "key-value" pairing structure. Reading input field labels from the Properties files requires the JSP developer to know each field label's corresponding key value. The JSP developer uses the key to find the label. The value is the textual label.

As shown in Figure 12-4, the "key" component is on the left side of the equation and the "value" component is on the right. In this example, the Java API reads a Properties file named address.properties and uses the key "NAME" to get the value "Name." The line beginning with "#" is a comment line that, in this example, tells the JSP developer that the key-value pairs are for address input field labels.

```
#address labels for input fields
#key=value
NAME=Name
ADDRESS=Address
CITY=City
STATE=State
ZIP=Zip Code
```

Figure 12-4: Properties File address.properties

Internationalization

Properties files are extremely useful when a Web application displays in multiple languages. When a Web application is internationalized, a group of Properties files can hold the same text in multiple languages. To accomplish this, a Properties file needs to be created for every language that the Web application is to support.

When a Web application has multiple language Properties files, these files need to be uniquely identified so that the correct version can be read. A standard technique to accomplish this is to add a language identifier as part of the Properties file name. For example, the name address_en.properties would identify an English version of our address Properties file and the name address_es.properties would identify a Spanish version. Looking at the language indicators, a JSP developer would know which version of the files is English and which version is Spanish. Figure 12-5 shows both the English and Spanish versions of the address Properties files.

```
#English properties file address_en.properties
#address labels for input fields
NAME=Name
ADDRESS=Address
CITY=City
STATE=State
ZIP=Zip Code

#Spanish properties file address_es.properties
#Address labels for input fields
NAME=Nombre
ADDRESS=Dirección
CITY=Ciudad
STATE=Estado
ZIP=Código Postal
```

Figure 12-5: Internationalized Properties File

The above example requires only one JSP to display a Web page in multiple languages. The JSP will read either the English or the Spanish version of the Properties file based upon the user's language preference, which is included in the HTTP request. When a HTTP request is sent to the JSP indicating a language preference, the Java program searches for a Properties file with the user's language preference and, if found, displays the content in the requested language. Otherwise, a default language Properties file is used. Since developers typically are not language translators, professional language translators are needed to convert the Properties files to the required language versions.

Additional Properties File Uses

Properties files reside on the J2EE application server and JSP developers can find many uses for them beyond the simple examples presented here.

One option may be to use a Properties file to store the content for a Help Contact page. This page may only contain a statement saying if you need help, please contact our help desk at this telephone number and this email address. A Web page like this does not seem to justify the effort to access this content from a relational database and hard coding should rarely be an option since the contact information may change. Reading the Help content from a Properties files would seem like the way to go.

Another option for using Properties files could be to use them for system configuration data. For example, a Properties file can contain data that configures an application's JDBC connection to a relational database.

Properties files are a powerful feature for any application to use that runs on a J2EE application server. Properties files can be created before the JSPs, discouraging JSP developers from hard coding the field labels within the JSPs. In addition, Web page designers or business analysts can create Properties files instead of tying up your Java developers to create them.

CHAPTER 13

Development Summary

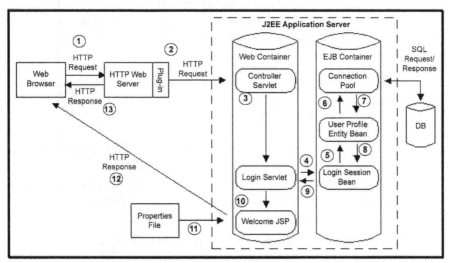

Figure 13-1: Our Example J2EE Application Flow

The previous chapters explained many of the technologies used to develop J2EE Web applications. The following pages provide a summary of how all of these technologies work together.

Summarized Development Chapter Flow

J2EE applications are based on HTTP request-response flows. When a user submits a URL using a Web browser, it is sent through a series of routers, servers, and processes before the requested Web page is returned to the browser. Figure 13-1 represents a HTTP request-response flow sequence for logging into the example Web application. (The numbers in Figure 13-1 correspond to the list number on the following pages.)

1. The Web browser submits a HTTP request to log onto the Web application. As shown in Figure 13-2, the request contains the following data: the Form action that tells our Web application to execute the ControllerServlet; the Form method that specifies a method type of post; the User ID and Password entered by the user; and, the hidden field BusinessServlet containing the value LoginServlet.

```
<html>
Log In to Our Application<br/><br/>
<form method="post" action="../servlet/ControllerServlet">
User ID: <input type="text" name="login_userid" size="10"/><br/>
Password: <input type="password" name="login_password" size="10"/>
<input type="hidden" name="BusinessServlet" value="LoginServlet"/>
<input type="submit" value="Submit"/>
</form>
</html>
```

Figure 13-2: HTML submits HTTP Request

2. The HTTP request arrives at the HTTP Web server, which determines that the request is for the ControllerServlet. The HTTP Web server uses the XML configured plug-in to pass the request to the J2EE application server for processing. The J2EE application server forwards the request to the Web container.

3. The Web container creates the Request and Response objects. The Request object stores information passed in the HTTP request and the response object stores the information passed in the HTTP response back to the Web browser.

   The Web container reads the Form's action and method type, causing it to execute the ControllerServlet's doPost method. In this method, the Java code:

   o Gets access to the Request object and Response object;

   o Creates the Session object;

   o Uses the value (e.g., LoginServlet) in the BusinessServlet to determine the Business Area Servlet to be executed; and

   o Writes the User ID and Password sent in the HTTP request to the Session object.

   The code in the ControllerServlet then initiates the execution of the LoginServlet code. (Figure 13-3)

```
import javax.servlet.*;
import javax.servlet.http.*;
public class ControllerServlet extends HttpServlet {
    public void doPost(HttpServletRequest request, HttpServletResponse response) {
        HttpSession session = request.getSession(true);
        if ("LoginServlet".equals(request.getParameter ("BusinessServlet") ) ) {
            session.setAttribute("s_userid", request.getParameter("login_userid") );
            session.setAttribute("s_password", request.getParameter("login_password") );
        }
        response.sendRedirect("../servlet/LoginServlet");
    }
}
```

Figure 13-3 : ControllerServlet executes LoginServlet

4. The LoginServlet controls the business process logic for logging into the Web application. Similar to the ControllerServlet, the Web container executes the LoginServlet's doPost method. In this method, the Java code gets access to the Request object, Response object, and the Session object created in the ControllerServlet. In addition, this method contains code for connecting the LoginServlet with the Login Session bean located in the EJB container. Once the connection occurs, the Login Session bean's compareUseridPwd method executes by passing it the User ID and Password that were initially stored in the Session object by the ControllerServlet. (Figure 13-4)

```
import javax.servlet.*;
import javax.servlet.http.*;
public class LoginServlet extends HttpServlet {
    public void doPost(HttpServletRequest request, HttpServletResponse response) {
        HttpSession session = request.getSession(false);
    Object homeObject = jndiContext.lookup("ejb/Login");
    LoginHome loginHome = (LoginHome)
            (javax.rmi.PortableRemoteObject.narrow(homeObject,LoginHome.class));
    Login loginobject = loginHome.create();
    int compareUseridPwd = loginobject.loginUser
            (session.getValue("s_userid").toString(),
             session.getValue("s_password").toString());
        ...
        ...
        }
    }
}
```

Figure 13-4 : LoginServlet executes Login Session bean's loginUser method

5. The Login Session bean compares the Password sent in the HTTP request against the Password stored in our application's relational database. To do this, the Login Session bean initiates the execution of the UserProfile Entity bean to get the previously stored Password from the database. (Figure 13-5)

```
import javax.ejb.*;
public class LoginBean implements SessionBean {
    public int loginUser(String enteredUserid, String enteredPassword) {
        Object homeObject = jndiContext.lookup
            (mySessionCtx.getEnvironment().getProperty("LOOKUP_NAME_USER-
            PROFILE"));
        UserProfileHome userobject = (UserProfileHome)
            (javax.rmi.PortableRemoteObject.narrow(homeObject,UserProfileHome.
            class));
        ...
        ...
    }
}
```

Figure 13-5 : Login Session bean executes UserProfile Entity bean's findByKey method

6. The UserProfile Entity bean uses the User ID in the HTTP request as the primary key to send a SQL request to the relational database to read a row (record) from the User Profile table. The findByKey method uses the User ID to retrieve a row containing this User ID as a primary key from the User Profile table. (Figure 13-6)

```
import javax.ejb.*;
public class LoginBean implements SessionBean {
        ...
        ...
        UserProfile userProfile = userobject.findByKey(enteredUserid);
        ...
        ...
        }
    }
}
```

Figure 13-6 : Login Session bean executes findByKey method

7. In this example, the SQL request is successful and finds the requested row in the User Profile table. The relational database sends a SQL response containing the stored Password back to the UserProfile Entity bean. Now the getPassword method shown in Figure 13-7 is able to access the Password that came from the User Profile table.

```
public class UserProfileBean implements EntityBean {
        public getPassword() {
                return password;
        }
}
```

Figure 13-7 : Login Session bean executes getPassword method

8. The Login Session Bean validates the Password sent in the HTTP request by comparing it against the Password read from the User Profile table by the UserProfile Entity bean. If the Passwords are equal, this bean returns a "1" to the LoginServlet, otherwise the bean returns a "2", meaning the passwords were not equal.
(Figure 13-8)

```
import javax.ejb.*;
public class LoginBean implements SessionBean {
        public int loginUser(String enteredUserid, String enteredPassword) {
                ...

                ...
                if (enteredPassword.equals(userProfile.getPassword())) {
                        return 1;     // passwords are the same
                else
                        return 2;     // passwords are different
                }
        }
}
```

Figure 13-8 : Login Session bean executes getPassword method

9. In the LoginServlet, the Password comparison return value (e.g., 1) is stored in the Java variable compareUseridPwd. (Figure 13-9)

```
import javax.servlet.*;
import javax.servlet.http.*;
public class LoginServlet extends HttpServlet {
    public void doPost(HttpServletRequest request, HttpServletResponse response) {
            HttpSession session = request.getSession(false);
        ...

        ...
        int compareUseridPwd = loginobject.loginUser
                    (session.getValue("s_userid").toString(),
                    session.getValue("s_password").toString());
        ...
        ...
    }
}
```

Figure 13-9: LoginServlet stores Passowrd comparison result

10. The LoginServlet uses compareUseridPwd to see if the returned value is a "1". If so, the servlet executes the Welcome JSP. (Figure 13-10)

```
import javax.servlet.*;
import javax.servlet.http.*;
public class LoginServlet extends HttpServlet {
    public void doPost(HttpServletRequest request, HttpServletResponse response) {
        HttpSession session = request.getSession(false);

        ...

        ...

        if (compareUseridPwd == 1) {
            response.sendRedirect("../jsp/Welcome.jsp");
        }
    }
}
```

Figure 13-10: LoginServlet executes Welcome JSP

11. When the Welcome JSP executes, it reads a Properties file for required Web content contained in that file. As the JSP executes, it merges any dynamically generated content with its static HTML tags.

12. The executed JSP returns as a HTTP response to the Web browser and displays as a Web page.

13. Have you ever noticed a Web page with lots of graphics, you will see the textual content of a Web page drawn in the browser first and then the images start appearing afterwards? This is because a Web server or J2EE application server sends the Web page's textual content to the Web browser first and then the browser sends additional HTTP requests for the images. If the images are stored on the J2EE application server, each image request is sent individually to the HTTP Web server which passes the request through the Web plug-in to the J2EE application server to find the images. For this reason, many dynamic Web applications store their images on the HTTP Web server. This way, instead of accessing the J2EE application server for each required image, the image file requests need only go to the Web server, saving response time and J2EE application server resources.

This concludes the discussion on some of the technologies developers use when writing code for a J2EE application. Once a Web application is developed, the code must be able to run on the J2EE application server. Chapter 14 explains how to package and deploy application code onto a J2EE application server.

CHAPTER 14

Deployment

For applications to execute on a J2EE application server, developers need to install, or deploy, the code onto the server. Deployment consists of the activities involved in getting a J2EE application installed and running in its operational environment. This chapter explains the terminology used in the deployment of the Java Servlet, EJB, and JSP components of a J2EE application.

Deployment involves the use of three different code packaging file types: the Enterprise application archive file (EAR), the Web application archive file (WAR), and the Enterprise JavaBean JAR (EJB JAR) file.

Enterprise Application Archive File

Developing J2EE applications requires the creation and reuse of thousands of lines of Java, HTML and XML code. To simplify the process of deploying an application onto a J2EE application server, J2EE provides for the packaging of the entire application into a single compressed file for deployment. This all-encompassing file is the Enterprise application archive (EAR) file.

The EAR file is the topmost file in a hierarchy of archive files. It can contain all of the archive files required for deployment of the application. The EAR file ends with a file type of ".ear" instead of the JAR file type of ".jar".

An EAR file contains many different file types used to deploy an application where JAR files mainly contain Java class files. To create an EAR file, the developer packages the Web application's code into two primary types of archive files that will be contained within the EAR file. These files are the Web application archive file and the EJB JAR file.

Web Application Archive File

The Web application archive (WAR) file contains the application code that executes within the Web container. The WAR file ends with a file type of ".war" and contains the many different file types used to build a Web application.

This code includes Java Servlets, JSPs, Properties files, and HTML files. The WAR file contains the View and Controller components of the MVC design used in the example application.

For example, in Figure 14-1 the WAR file contains a Controller Servlet, Login Servlet, Welcome JSP, and Properties file. (Since HTML files are static in nature, you might want to serve them from the HTTP Web server instead of the Java application server. If that were the case, you would not include them in the WAR file.)

Enterprise JavaBean JAR File

The EJB JAR file contains the application code that executes within the EJB container and ends with a file type of ".jar". The EJB code includes the Entity Beans and Session Beans. In the example application, the EJB file contains the Model components of the MVC design. As Figure 14-1 illustrates, the example application has an EJB JAR file containing the Login Session Bean and User Profile Entity Bean files.

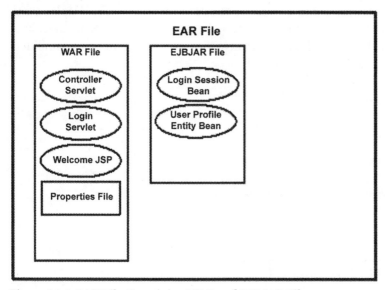

Figure 14-1: EAR File Containing WAR and EJB JAR Files

Deployment Descriptors

When a developer deploys the EAR file onto a J2EE application server, the application server needs to understand what is contained in the EAR, WAR and EJB JAR files. This is accomplished using a special configuration file called a Deployment Descriptor file. A Deployment Descriptor is an XML file that is used to specify application code and container behavior when the Web application is deployed.

J2EE applications use the Deployment Descriptor to tell the J2EE application server what the EAR, WAR and EJB JAR files contain and how to deploy each of these files. The EAR, WAR, and EJB JAR files each have their own version of a Deployment Descriptor with specific information about that file.

For example, an EAR Deployment Descriptor tells the application server which WAR and EJB JAR files it contains, while an EJB JAR Deployment Descriptor tells the application server which Session Beans are stateful beans and which are stateless.

EAR File Deployment Descriptors

As previously stated, one of the functions of the EAR file Deployment Descriptor is to identify the WAR and EJB JAR files contained within the EAR file. To create this Deployment Descriptor, a developer creates the file as an XML file. For the example Web application, the EAR file Deployment Descriptor contains an entry for one WAR file, yourWebSiteName.war, and one EJB JAR, myEjb.jar. These two archive files are listed as modules contained in the EAR file as shown in Figure 14-2.

```
<application id="Application_ID">
    <module id="EjbModule_999999">
        <ejb>myEjb.jar</ejb>
    </module>
    <module id="WebModule_999999">
        <web>
            <web-uri>yourWebSiteName.war</web-uri>
        </web>
    </module>
</application>
```

Figure 14-2: EAR File Deployment Descriptor

Each Deployment Descriptor is stored within its respective EAR, WAR and EAR JAR file, and each Deployment Descriptor has a special name. The Deployment Descriptor file for the EAR file is called "application.xml" since it contains the entire application components being deployed on the J2EE application server. The WAR file contains the components deployed within the Web container, so its Deployment Descriptor file is named "web.xml". The EJB JAR file is deployed in the EJB container, so its Deployment Descriptor file is named "ejb-jar.xml". Figure 14-3 shows the Deployment Descriptors added to their respective EAR, WAR and EJB JAR files.

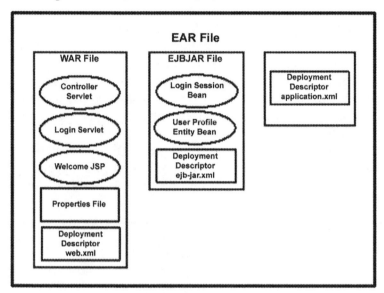

Figure 14-3: EAR File with Deployment Descriptors

A note about the deployment of Java API JAR files: If a Web application contains Java API JAR files, e.g., the log4j.jar file, they will also be contained within the EAR file. Typically, Java API JAR files are stored as part of the WAR file since these files are typically used by the JSPs and Java Servlets.

Multiple Code Deployments

When a developer first deploys an EAR file, its initial target is not the production J2EE application server. In fact, a development team can use multiple J2EE application servers during the course of developing and testing a J2EE application.

For example, a development team usually develops their pieces of the Web application on their individual workstations. When the team is ready to integrate and test everyone's application code, the team typically deploys the code onto a development J2EE application server, which simulates the eventual production server. The development team uses the development server to do all their integration and final testing for their application code. As such, the development server is in a constant state of change.

When the application is ready for the user community to test, the development team deploys the EAR file to a test J2EE application server. This gives the user community a stable environment to test the application. If user testing discovers any issues with the application, the development team corrects the issues on their workstations and re-deploys the code on the development server for integration testing. After successfully testing the code, the team promotes and re-deploys the code back onto the test server for the users to test again.

This test-and-fix sequence continues until the user community says the application is functioning correctly. If the project team has used OOA/D techniques along with reusing a lot of existing open source code, the user testing cycle should not take long.

Once the application is tested and given the green light for operational deployment, the Web application runs on the production J2EE application server. Figure 14-4 illustrates deploying the EAR file to these three J2EE application servers.

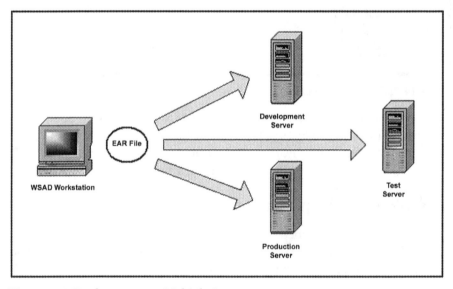

Figure 14-4: Deployments on Multiple Servers

Version Control

When deploying application code, especially with the multiple deployments that are part of any J2EE project, it is essential to ensure the correct version of the code is used. The very nature of J2EE projects require many tasks be done in parallel and that version control is essential during development when the application code is being created. Ensuring that the correct version of code is worked on can be especially complicated when the development team is situated in different locations, possibly different parts of the world, which has become increasingly common for projects. As such, it is important to employ a version control system that tracks the history of changes made to application code and allows developers to store and access the version of code they need, especially from remote locations using the Internet.

A popular version control system that is used on many J2EE projects is the open source Concurrent Versions System® (CVS). CVS provides a central repository that can store both application code and project documentation. CVS allows developers to track changes to their source code, ensuring that they are working on the correct version of the code. When used for storing project documentation, the project team can use CVS to track all versions of the documentation including project specifications, UML diagrams, test cases, project plans, status reports, and project change requests. Using CVS helps ensures that the latest version of anything about the project is stored in one central place, eliminating the risk of multiple versions of documentation or code stored on many computers.

Your team can download CVS from the Internet at no charge. A common place to install the CVS repository is on a development server where developers typically have greater control of the server. Regardless of where the CVS repository is installed, it can be accessed over the Internet making it available to project team members from anywhere in the world.

There are different ways that the project team can access CVS. Integrated Java development environments like IBM's WebSphere Studio Application Developer® (WSAD) have built-in capabilities for accessing the CVS repository. For project team members that are not developers and do not have access to tools like WSAD, there are other CVS access options:

o Use a Unix command prompt for entering CVS commands that store and retrieve project documentation. This is not an easy option for non-technical members who are not familiar with using a Unix command prompt.

o Use a CVS GUI front-end tool that can access the CVS repository. This makes CVS much easier to use than a Unix command prompt. There is a very good open source CVS GUI tool called WinCVS® that is also available to download at no charge.*

---

* To obtain more information about CVS, visit http://www.cvshome.org/ and for more information regarding WinCVS, go to http://www.wincvs.org/.

Figure 14-5 illustrates a project team employing version control using WSAD and WinCvs to access the CVS repository.

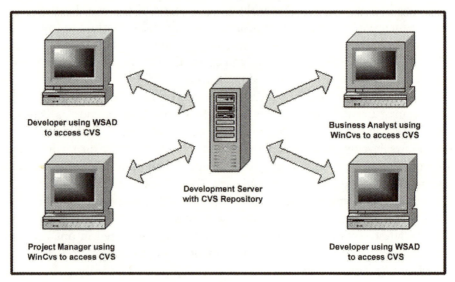

Figure 14-5: Accessing the CVS Repository

CHAPTER 15

FINAL THOUGHTS

The purpose of this book is to provide project managers and non-developer project team members a high-level understanding of the technologies involved in building a J2EE application and how the technologies interact. In an effort to keep the book brief, it only touches on the core technologies involved in the building a J2EE application.

It is important to understand that developers work with a number of technologies when developing a J2EE application. Figure 15-1 provides a list containing many of the technologies that a J2EE developer needs to understand just to build the example application shown in this book.

o Concurrent VersionsSystem (CVS)	o Enterprise JavaBeans (EJB)
o eXtensible Hypertext Markup Language (XHTML)	o Hypertext Markup Language (HTML)
o Hypertext Transfer Protocol (HTTP)	o Internet Protocol (IP)
o Java	o Java 2 Platform Enterprise Edition (J2EE)
o Java archive (JAR)	o J2EE Application Server
o Java DataBase Connectivity (JDBC)	o Java Servlet
o JavaServer Page (JSP)	o Structured Query Language (SQL)
o Deployment Descriptor	o eXtensive Markup Language (XML)
o Object-Oriented Analysis (OOA)	o Object-Oriented Design (OOD)
o Object-Oriented Programming (OOP)	o Relational Data Base Management System (RDBMS)
o Unified Modeling Language (UML)	o HTTP Web Server

Figure 15-1: Listing of Technologies Mentioned in this Book

The technologies presented in this book are just a subset of the technologies that could be involved in developing a J2EE application. Figure 15-2 contains a list of additional technologies that J2EE developers might need to understand when developing a J2EE application. This list is not even a comprehensive list of technologies that can be involved in developing these type applications.

o Cascading Stylesheets (CSS)	o Dynamic HTML (DHTML)
o Document Type Definition (DTD)	o eXtensible Stylesheet Language (XSL)
o eXtensible Stylesheet Language Transformations (XSLT)	o Interface Definition Language (IDL)
o Internet Inter-ORB Protocol (IIOP)	o JavaBeans
o Java Message Service (JMS)	o Java Naming and Directory Interface (JNDI)
o JavaMail	o Java Transaction API (JTA)
o Java Transaction Service (JTS)	o JavaServer Pages (JSP) Standard Tag Library (JSTL)
o Lightweight Directory Access Protocol (LDAP)	o Javascript
o Remote Method Invocation (RMI)	o UNIX shell scripts, editors and commands

Figure 15-2: List of Additional Technologies

There is also numerous vendor-specific development and deployment software products that J2EE developers need to be know. Figure 15-3 is a list of some the IBM-specific products that can be used in analyzing, designing, developing and deploying a J2EE application.

o Rational for object-oriented analysis, design and testing	o IBM HTTP Server (IHS) for the Web server
o AIX for unix operating system	o DB2 for relational database management system
o WebSphere Application Server (WAS) for Java application server	o WebSphere Studio Application Developer (WSAD) for Java integrated development environment

Figure 15-3 IBM Products

While this overview did not discuss the benefits of developers using integrated development tools, these tools have a positive impact on the quality, speed and ease of developing application code. An integrated Java development environment like WSAD provides developers a powerful tool for developing J2EE Web applications. Using WSAD, developers can develop Java Servlets, EJBs, JSPs, HTML, and XML, test the code, and then package the code into the EAR file for deployment to a J2EE application server.

As you can see, the development world has become much more robust and complex for J2EE developers. There are many technologies involved in a project's development processes and different vendor products that they need to understand how to use. We hope that after reading this book, you have a basic understanding of the skills and technologies developers use when designing, developing and deploying J2EE applications.

As with J2EE developers, we believe the role of project managers has become much more complicated. With the increasing complexity of creating J2EE Web applications, it has become much more difficult to manage projects without an understanding of what is involved in developing the applications. This is true on any project, but especially true whenever a project becomes troubled.

The source of troubled projects is generally not technical, but when technical issues are involved, managers need to be able to understand what is going on as the technical team explains the issues and the options for solving or working around them. Without this understanding, it is much more difficult to make the decisions needed to get—and keep—the project on track.

As a project manager, there is no problem relying on others to help make the technical decisions. That is what your project architect does for you. It is beneficial, however, for a project manager to understand the big picture of the overall technologies involved as this knowledge can help guide a pressured team through the tough decisions the team may need to make. As developers, we appreciate a manager who understands the big picture on our projects.

In summary, this book may have not explained all the technologies that you need to know to work with your team, but we hope it has given you a solid base for building your knowledge of J2EE applications. On behalf of developers everywhere, we appreciate that you have taken the time and effort to learn more about the technologies involved in developing J2EE Web applications.

978-0-595-36979-9
0-595-36979-0

www.ingramcontent.com/pod-product-compliance
Lightning Source LLC
Chambersburg PA
CBHW051253050326
40689CB00007B/1178